"A LIGHTHEARTED ROMP THROUGH A TYPICAL SEASON . . . MR. GEIST HAS A GIFT FOR UNCOVERING THE QUIRKY DETAIL THAT MAKES THE MUNDANE HUMOROUS . . . ESSENTIAL READING FOR SEASONS TO COME."

—*The New York Times Book Reveiw*

The critics love

LITTLE LEAGUE CONFIDENTIAL
by Bill Geist

The best seller everyone's talking about

"WONDERFUL . . . filled with empathy for kids, impatience for pushy parents, and a good sense of humor."
—*Booklist*

"Geist does an expert job of creating humor out of the chaos of managing squads of unfocused kids."
—*Time*

"A FUNNY BOOK . . . there are wonderful moments culled from the season, and most of them are bizarre enough to be true."—*Chicago Tribune*

"AN HONEST AND HILARIOUS LOOK at Little League baseball from a coach's point of view."

—*Pasedena Star-News*

"Geist has a sure touch, a keen eye for foibles."

—*Newsday* (N.Y.)

"Takes its readers on a laughter-filled journey through a season of America's favorite pastime from tryouts to the Ridgewood World Series."

—*Lexington Herald-Leader*

"A HILARIOUS ACCOUNT of Little League baseball . . . full of witty observations."

—*Library Journal*

"SIDE-SPLITTING . . . for anyone in need of a good laugh."

—*Publishers Weekly*

Books by Bill Geist

THE ZUCCHINI PLAGUE AND OTHER
TALES OF SUBURBIA

CITY SLICKERS

LITTLE LEAGUE CONFIDENTIAL

One Coach's Completely Unauthorized Tale of Survival

BILL GEIST

A Dell Book

Published by
Dell Publishing
a division of
Bantam Doubleday Dell Publishing Group, Inc.
1540 Broadway
New York, New York 10036

ISBN: 0-440-21506-4

Reprinted by arrangement with Macmillan Publishing Company

Printed in the United States of America

Published simultaneously in Canada

June 1993

10 9 8 7 6 5 4 3 2 1

OPM

For Willie and Libby

ACKNOWLEDGMENTS

Acknowledgments?

Let's see. I acknowledge that in the beginning the earth was without form and void. I acknowledge the duly elected government of Canada, the pedestrian's (theoretical) right of way, and the final authority of the President of the World Wrestling Federation, without which there would be chaos.

More relevantly, I want to give special thanks to Abner Doubleday who inven . . . He didn't?! Well, that makes it complete. Now, *everything* I learned in school has been invalidated.

Thanks to Claire Chiappetta, who definitely did produce the CBS television piece we did on my daughter's baseball team for the *Sunday Morning with Charles Kuralt* show, which inspired this book. Thanks to Charles Kuralt and to Linda Mason, executive producer, for airing it.

Thanks most of all to Tom Connor, who saw the piece, came up with the big idea to make a book out of it, and saw it through—and through, and through. (Keep fighting for that open bar at the book party, Tom).

Thanks to all those at Macmillan, especially Rick Wolff, the former minor league baseball player, now major league editor. Finally, an editor with a sense of humor! But then, he'd have to have one, wouldn't he, to pay me for this book?

Thanks for the rich material to all my co-coaches and all my players—also to my opponents and my players' parents, often one and the same.

Thanks to my wife, Jody, and, of course, to my son, Willie, and my daughter, Libby, for seeing me through my difficult Little League years. I'm better now, thanks.

—Bill Geist

LITTLE LEAGUE CONFIDENTIAL

Hello, Andy? This is Mr. Geist, Willie's father. I called to tell you that I'm going to be your baseball coach this year.

Um-hm.

Our first practice is Thursday, four o'clock, on the diamond behind Ben Franklin School.

Um-hm.

Say Andy, I wanted you to know—and we can keep this just between the two of us, OK?—that you were the first player I picked for my team! They told me you were on the all-star team last year!

Oh, yeh, that was my brother, Adam.

What?

Yeh. He's great. I. . . I don't really care much for sports myself.

(Pause.) Ah, c'mon, Andy, sure you do.

(Silence.)

See you Thursday, Adam.

Andy.

Yeah, Andy.

Hello, is your brother home?

I don't have a brother.

Well, is Gene there?

This is Jean.

(Pause.) So, uh, Jean. You're a . . . girl.

Yes.

That's interesting, interesting.

Hello, Neville. Say, you have the same name as the mayor.

He's my dad.

Oh, great.

I don't have to play outfield again this year, do I coach?

Well, Neville, all the players on our team will be playing lots of different positions, we want to give everyone a chan—

The coach made me play the outfield all last sea-

son, and my dad got so mad he said he was going to send the tax assessor over to his house.

(Pause.) Oh! Well, Neville, I'm sure you'll be playing *a lot* of infield. (Christ! The new kitchen!!!) By the way, Neville, what is your very *favorite* position?

Hello, Hermie?

Oh, hello, Mr. Geist. Enjoyed your piece in Sunday's Times *on the changing political situation in Botswana.*

Well, thanks Herm, but, that wasn't mine, actually. You're interested in Botswana?

I take an interest in everything. My compliments to the writer.

Hello, is Lynn at home?

No, I'm afraid not. This is her mother.

(Pause.) So, um, she's a girl too?

What do you mean, "too"?

Also. (That bastard who coaches Jiffy Lube told me at the draft that Lynn was *definitely* a boy!)

Well, this better not conflict with ballet.

♦ ♦ ♦

Hello, Byron? I'm your coach this year, and—

Yeh. I heard. I heard. I think we got a good team this year, coach. Think we'll kick a little butt, know what I mean?

I'm sure we will. I hope we'll be kicking quite a bit, actually.

Good. Say, coach, let's get something straight. Don't call me Byron. Ever. I go by my initials, B.A., which also stand for "Bad Ass."

Um-hm.

Don't have any girls *on the team, do we, coach?*

Oh, heh-heh, you know how it is these days . . . maybe just a couple.

Too bad. Bottom of the ninth, bases loaded, two outs—you know what I'm talking about.

Sure, sure.

Do we finally get to lead off when we run the bases this year?

No, Bad A. . . no, I don't believe we do.

That really sucks, *doesn't it?*

Why, uh, yes, it certainly does. Suck.

Emily isn't home right now, she's over at the Agnew School triathlon.

Great! Swimming, running, biking?
No. Math, geography and violin.
Super.

I*'m glad you called. How did Danny get on* your *team? We specifically asked in a notarized letter that Danny be placed on Mr. Flint's team. They have a very close relationship, and Danny needs that kind of support. We have filed a formal complaint with The Commissioner of Baseball.*

Hi, Monique.
I don't know if I can play this year, Mr. Geist.
Why not?
I have Lee Press-On Nails.

(Dialing.) (Well, it looks like I've got two Andys this year.)
Eh-lo.
Hello, is this Andy?
No-no. Name is "Anand."
Excuse me?
Anand.

Your name is Ah-nahnd?

Yes I think so; we are from India.

Super. Super country. Well, welcome, welcome to this land . . . and, um, well: where in the heck did you learn to play baseball?

Sorry. I do not know this . . . bazebohl?

You're gonna love it.

Hello. My name is Bill. And I'm a Little League coach. I've been one for nine seasons, and I'm about to do it again.

I know it's bad for me sometimes, but I can't seem to stop.

Coaching, like smoking Camels and drinking stingers, is voluntary, of course. Waking one day to find yourself suddenly transformed into—Aieee!—A Little League Parent is not.

This book is written for The Few And The Many: for those few men and women who are remodeling my basement and demand to be paid; and for the many parents and coaches out there who, like myself, suffer from Little League Syndrome. Millions are afflicted.

How serious is LLS? Well, it can cause nervousness, dyspepsia and distemper. It can cause you to lose friends and make enemies, put a strain on family relationships and get you called into the boss's office for leaving work early a lot to attend practices and games.

Tragically, there are no support groups, no wing at the Betty Ford clinic. It hasn't even been written up in the *New England Journal of Medicine,* yet.

I see lesser stuff on *Donahue,* believe me.

I know the psychiatric community is aware of LLS, because a couple parents of my players talk about their symptoms on the couch. "I tell my shrink I'm like Jekyll and Hyde," confided Hermie's mother. "I turn into a monster at Little League games, and I can't stop myself." The sudden emergence of claws, hair on the back of her hands, frothing at the mouth. Not pretty.

I began coaching baseball nine years ago in Ridgewood, New Jersey; first my son's teams, now my daughter's. I played Little League baseball myself in Champaign, Illinois, for five years.

I have written for the *New York Times* about Little League baseball in Paramus, New Jersey, a typical suburb where the spectacle of Little League returns each spring as surely as potholes and patio furniture, replete with the perennial cheers and tears and debates over the philosophical merits of the competitive program—not to mention the debates over whether the coach's kid plays too much: "On opening day, the eight-year-old pitcher stands on the mound chewing an enormous wad of bubble gum and trying to look as menacing as possible—no mean feat when you're almost completely concealed by the steerhide of your baseball glove and your oversized baseball pants are billowing in the spring breeze like queen-sized sheets hung out to dry."

I have written about the establishment of Little League baseball on the trendy Upper West Side of Manhattan, where preseason questions included: would the uniforms be purchased at Charivari? Would the catcher be overcome by carbon monoxide fumes from rush hour traffic whizzing past fifteen feet behind the backstop? And would the winning team be treated not to the traditional postgame ice cream cones, but to Toffutti or gelato?

I covered for CBS News a Little League game in the Dominican Republic, where kids without benefit of gloves or shoes played on a crude diamond carved out of a sugar cane field and cows wandered around in short center field. (They tended to play somewhat better than their American counterparts, many of whom have a couple hundred dollars' worth of equipment.)

I have interviewed experts on why Taiwan kicks our collective butt almost every year in the Little League World Series, and the answer is that the kids from Taiwan work hours a day on fundamentals, every day, all year long. Now, kids from Florida and California and Arizona could certainly play baseball all year round, too, but there is soccer and the 7-Eleven and MTV and well, like, you know how it is in America.

Little League baseball is played in thirty-seven countries. And everywhere it is much the same. Somewhere in Zimbabwe, a father yells (in the Ndebele language): "Good eye, son. Good eye."

This book is strictly personal. The idea for the book grew out of a television piece I did on coaching one of my daughter's teams. The piece, which aired on *Sunday Morning with Charles Kuralt,* struck a chord with a lot of fellow sufferers, and was an Emmy Award finalist. I don't know if it won or not. It was put in a category with things like *Nelson Mandela, a Profile in Courage,* so I sensed *Little League Baseball* might not make it with the judges and I didn't pop for the tuxedo needed to attend the banquet. That was a couple of years ago, and I probably would have heard something by now.

Everything in this book happened. Because these are children—either by virtue of age or emotional development—names have been changed and some of the games and characters are composites drawn from my nine years of coaching.

These are litigious times, and the real estate market being what it is, I have to live in this town.

Play ball.

WILLIE

Willie couldn't wait. Two years before he was old enough to join Little League, he began playing imaginary games of baseball solitaire in the backyard.

I'd arrive home from work to hear his sweet voice wafting in through the kitchen window. Parting the curtain gently so as not to disturb the moment, I'd see him standing out there, holding his baseball cap over his heart, singing the national anthem.

After ". . . and the home of the Braves" (Atlanta presumably), Willie would resolutely tug on his cap and take the field, often to the crowd's roar, which he also furnished.

Sometimes I'd get home in time to hear him announce the starting lineups before the anthem. Living in the New York area, he imitated the rather sophisticated enunciation of the Yankee Stadium announcer, Bob Sheppard: "Bahting thihd, playing right field for the Yankees, nuhmbuh 31, Dave Winfield. Winfield."

Willie liked Winfield. On our vacations he used to write him postcards from Lake George and Cape Cod care of Yankee Stadium that began: "Dear Winfield . . ."

Willie pitched. He'd take the mound (a sandbox in the likeness of a turtle) and begin his warmup throws. He wouldn't actually let go of the ball because there was no catcher. His favorite part was giving the little flick of the glove that the pitcher makes just before he makes his last warmup pitch, to let the catcher know he should make his practice throw to second. He was already picking up the nuances of the game, his favorite part of baseball, and mine.

Before throwing that first pitch he'd always spit a couple of times—an aspect of his game that needed work (I'll spare you the details). Then he'd stare in at the imaginary catcher, shake off his first sign, nod his approval at the second and pretend to throw the ball.

Most of the time, the batters were defenseless against his blazing fastball and they simply struck out. Although, occasionally after throwing a pretend pitch, Willie would toss a ball into the air as if the batter had somehow managed to hit it, then he'd catch it for the out, sometimes heroically crashing into a wall of ivy after the catch. Or he might pick up the ball off the ground and throw it at the big oak tree, representing the first baseman. This always startled Bert, the cat, a regular attendee, perched on the picnic table, taking in the action. Once or twice during the game, Willie would even allow the opposition a hit, and sometimes a run.

But when Willie came to bat, look out. If the opposition scored, it would stir Willie to make a heroic comeback at the plate. He was sort of a Jose Canseco and Wade Boggs all rolled into one up there. If he didn't blast an imaginary monumental Canseco-style homer, he'd at least hit a Wade Boggs double, knocking in a couple of runs.

No matter what the hit, he always found it necessary to slide. Had to slide. Loved it. Loved the dirt. And he always beat the tag.

Even when he hit a ball completely out of the

imaginary stadium—over the roof!—he'd slide into home.

If there was so much as a trace of light remaining, I'd postpone dinner and join him. Willie was always ready to drop his fanciful game for a real game of catch: "Dad! Let's have a catch!" We'd throw the ball back and forth, back and forth, until late spring's twilight faded to black. Neither of us wanted to stop. It was sublime.

When Willie finally stepped to the plate for the first time in the Tiny Tim division of Little League, he looked over at his mother and me, hanging on the fence, and he smiled, confident as could be that he'd not only be hitting the ball, but he'd more than likely be hitting it a long, long way—just as he did in those imaginary games.

We, on the other hand, were nervous wrecks. I could never bring myself to have that little talk with Willie, pointing out that baseball is a game where you tend to fail more often than you succeed. Even Winfield. Who could bear to dampen the unbounded confidence and enthusiasm? But! It *has* been half a century now since anyone hit safely in even four out of ten at bats over an entire major league season, let alone hitting safely half the time.

Maybe Willie would be the one to do it. That's how fathers think. I knew what Willie expected to do; and feared he might be thinking that's what I expected of him too.

As he looked out at the pitcher, I told myself I would not be disappointed if he didn't hit the ball. It would be wrong—totally *unreasonable!*—to *expect* an eight-year-old to hit the ball in his first at bat. And yet . . .

How we felt for him. This was real life! Hardball! His first encounter with *real adversaries!* A whole *team* out there in the field, trying to make our little boy fail, trying to destroy his self-esteem, trying to make him cry!

The lovely game of baseball suddenly seemed terribly cruel. The all-American game. Maybe Lenin was right about this whole dog-eat-dog thing, you know?

There were *seven* outfielders out there. Count 'em. In this league, all the kids played all the time, so there wouldn't be any hurt feelings. Thirteen on a team: six infielders, *seven* outfielders. What about the *hitter's* feelings? *DiMaggio* couldn't get a hit against seven outfielders!

I had the urge to run out on the field, sweep up my little boy and take him *home!* Set him down gently amongst the dandelions in his own backyard, where we could play catch and where he could go on hitting those imaginary home runs and trotting around the basepaths to the cheers of adoring fans. . . forever.

Instead, here came the pitch, the first real pitch of his life.

Strike one?! Give me a break!

That ball was over his head! God, I hated that umpire.

I glanced at my wife to see how she was taking strike one. She was glaring at the umpire, an intense, menacing look I hadn't seen since I happened upon a mother bear in the woods with her cubs.

No longer a figure of speech: my wife wanted to actually Kill the Umpire! Had the biological imperative to Kill the Umpire, in order to protect her young.

The ump must have seen the "go-ahead-make-my-day" look she was giving him because the next pitch was in exactly the same place as the first and he called: "Ball one!"; and the one after that was "Ball two."

Fine, fine, OK.

A walk. I'd forgotten that Willie could simply . . . walk. What a wonderful way out of this whole traumatic situation. A *beautiful* solution, really, isn't it? A walk.

No dishonor. No hurt. A walk's as good as a hit, they say. I've heard people say that, haven't you? Takes a smart kid not to swing at bad pitches.

"Good eye," I shouted. "Good eye." I have since shouted that ten thousand times.

I . . . just . . . wanted . . . my . . . son . . . *safely* on first base.

That baseball term, "safe," suddenly took on a whole new depth of meaning.

The next pitch came floating slowly toward the plate, looking pretty good as it came closer, like it just might be strike two, when: Willie took a swing.

There was a "plink," the sound of an aluminum bat hitting . . . the ball. Hitting it!

And there it went, the ball heading to the right side, a ground ball, a fair ball, headed in the general direction of the second baseman, but maybe just to the right of the second baseman, actually. But, so *slowly*. Would it get to that space before the second baseman?

It looked like a routine out, really. But wait! Adjust the thinking! This was not the TV Game of the Week. And this was not Ryne Sandberg playing second base. It was just some little kid who might well blow it.

Go, ball, go! The ball was going to make it just into the grass in right field. Yes!

We looked back at Willie, still standing in the batter's box, looking a bit stunned, and still innocent to the dangers posed by real adversaries in the field.

"Run!" I screamed.

"Run, Willie!" shrieked his mother.

Willie shot a look at us.

"Run!"

And, fear in his eyes, our little boy began to run.

EARLY ON

It begins early. At Little League games, some fathers have admitted—or mothers have happily testified as hostile witnesses against them—that among the first thoughts they had after learning they were fathers-to-be was a vision of playing catch with their sons in the backyard. And, yes, all right, if need be, with their *daughters.*

"Honey, did that sonogram indicate if the kid is a lefty or a righty? I was in the sporting goods store today . . ."

The mother of a particularly talented Little League shortstop—a boy I grew to despise as he robotically and errorlessly vacuumed up my son's ground balls and threw him out at first—told me that her husband used to put a portable radio tuned to Mets games up to her stomach when she was pregnant to imprint an interest in baseball on the yet unborn. It seemed a calculated risk. I mean, the kid could be walking around saying "Less Filling! Tastes Great!" the rest of his life, too.

"He was kidding," she said, "I think. He did it a lot."

I told her that was really silly, that I'd waited until the moment of birth, bringing a Rawlings catcher's mitt to the delivery room for use by the obstetrician. Curiously, however, the baby turned out to be a first baseman. Go figure.

Of one thing most expectant fathers are certain: their kid is going to get a much earlier start on the game than they did, a leg up, a competitive advantage. We fathers were never as good at the game as we wanted to be—let alone as good as we told our children we were.

Expectant fathers worry that their offspring will inherit their mediocre hand-eye coordination, their short legs, their clumsy feet. What if my son hates baseball and joins the Audio-Visual Club? What if: My son is a girl? It can happen. It happened to me once.

The first indication of athletic prowess seized upon by fathers with LLS is the newborn's APGAR score, a score from one to ten given immediately after the birth to indicate the child's overall health. If the score is a nine or a ten, fathers immediately start thinking: professional triple-A ball or higher; something in the six or seven range might mean the best the kid can do is make the high school team. Any score lower than that, and fathers' thoughts naturally turn to adoption.

If the father *protests* the APGAR score, suing the hospital to upgrade it, he has the makings of a Little League coach!

I bought Willie one of those little baseball uniforms for newborns, the pinstriped ones with the little caps. He looked just like a little Yankee or perhaps a Cub, except for the large patch of drool on his chest.

"Did you *see* that?!" my wife would shriek, indicating I should punish my son for hitting his grandmother with a stick.

"Yes, I did," I'd answer. "He showed good hand-eye coordination that time, but I truly believe he'd develop more power through the hitting zone if he'd step toward her and extend those arms."

And when she called the office to tell me the baby had just chucked a piece of Waterford across the dining room, I'd say: "All the way across? Was it on an arc or more of a clothesline throw? How about the accuracy?" She'd hang up.

When he could sit up a little bit, at least when propped, we played a little "catch." It was sort of like one of those carnival midway games: I'd toss a tiny little ball and see if it would come to rest on a roll of fat or a protrusion of some kind, somewhere on his person. When it did, I'd haul out the camcorder.

I figured when the kid could stand, he was ready for batting practice. I bought the Biiiiig, fat, red plastic bat at K-Mart and the really Biiiiig white plastic ball, to get Willie in the swing of things. The technique I recommend is getting on your knees about three feet away (just far enough to not get hit by the Biiiiig bat), yell "Swing!" then toss the ball where the bat might be. (You determine this by having the child take several practice swings.) If! the child hits the ball or even swings the bat, you cheer wildly. But don't worry, you will, you will. However, there are other fathers who eschew positive reinforcement, preferring to touch the kid lightly with a cattle prod when he misses. Your call.

♦ ♦ ♦

Another daydream I had when my wife was pregnant was taking my son to a major league game. Here, fathers also tend to jump the gun a bit. Last year a Bostonian in the stands at the Red Sox spring training camp in Florida held his—snoozing—six-month-old son and said to me: "I just had to bring him down so he could *see* this."

In my daydream, my unborn son would be sitting there in a blue baseball cap slightly askew or pulled down too far on his head, his little legs dangling, not long enough to reach the ground. He is wearing his little baseball glove on one hand and eating a hot dog with the other, chewing on the ends of both glove and dog. The weather is perfect, of course, sunny and mild, about seventy-six degrees. Our seats are very good. The home team is winning. My son adores me. My tie is loosened, my sleeves are rolled up, and I am (somehow) handsome.

Unfortunately, we lived on the North Side of Chicago when my son was a toddler, so the first game he saw was a Cubs game at Wrigley Field. I know of no finer place to watch a baseball game, although many of us have come to realize that raising a child to be a Cubs fan is a particularly heinous form of child abuse—with lifelong consequences.

Back in Illinois in 1955, my grandfather told me that, well, sure, it had been ten long years since the Cubs had won a pennant but that—doggone it!—I should show some loyalty and stick with 'em! (We lived equidistant between Chicago and St. Louis and I was entertaining the idea of a switch to the Cardinals.) My grandfather was lucky. He died that year. Thirty-seven years later, I'm still waiting for the Cubs to do something.

The reality of taking my son to a ballgame was somewhat less idyllic than the daydream. The home team, as is its custom, was not winning.

And this being Chicago, and the month May, the weather was not *quite* perfect. It wasn't bad for *Chicago,* I mean the airport wasn't closed, yet, but it was drizzling a bit, the temperature just warm enough to keep the rain from solidifying. Hell, this was a nice day, springtime in Chicago—time to haul out the lawn furniture.

Willie loved the food. He consumed one hot dog, one bag of peanuts, one box of popcorn, one coke and one ice cream bar in the first five innings. It was not the last we'd see of it.

He asked for, and received, a Cubs cap, pennant and T-shirt. Counting my three beers and hot dog, the afternoon cost just under the Blue Book value of our Datsun wagon.

Midway through the game, the light drizzle turned to rain. But! The Cubs were playing the Padres, and the San Diego chicken saved the day for Willie by running and sliding headfirst across the tarpaulin. By the time the rain delay was over, Willie was asleep. He awakened after the last pitch of the game, and asked: "Did the Cubs win, Dad?"

"Uh, why, yes, son, yes they did," I answered. Falsely.

Some fathers want to take their kids to ballgames because it reminds them so much of what they did with their own fathers. Not me. I don't think I ever went to a baseball game with my father. We lived in a small town; to go to a baseball game you had to go all the way to Chicago, and no one in his right mind went to Chicago, a city filled with unspeakable traffic and hoodlums—not to mention Democrats! I don't want to say we were provincial, but our high school foreign exchange student was from . . . America. Hawaii.

I have fond memories of lying on the top bunk of the bed I shared with my brother, David, listening to Cardinals baseball games (and Cubs away games) on the radio in the dark while he gently bounced me off the ceiling. Harry Carey, Joe Garagiola and Jack Buck did the Cardinals' broadcasts. There is something wonderful about listening to a baseball game on the radio in the dark.

My brothers-in-law have similar memories of listening to ballgames on summer evenings on the porch in Indianapolis with their grandfather, who was always smoking a cigar. For the moment to be absolutely perfect, the game had to be an obscure one: maybe the Indians and the Orioles.

I met a man in Chicago who loved listening to night games on the radio. He was a lifelong Tigers fan, who had been (tragically) transferred to Chicago at about age fifty. He'd put on his pajamas and drive to the western shore of Lake Michigan, where if he got his car lined up at just the right angle he could pick up Ernie Harwell's broadcasts from Tiger Stadium.

I tried doing that with Willie some, on our screened-in porch in Chicago, and he liked it all right, I guess, but after a while he would always say: "The game's on TV, Daddy."

I know, son, I know.

TRYING OUT

In January, Tony the mailman slips up our icy wooden steps, slides across the porch and delivers a stack of lingering Christmas bills.

Buried in their midst is the highly unseasonable notice from Commissioner Foozle's office notifying citizens that it's time once again to sign up the kids for Little League baseball.

It brings a shiver, just the thought of being outside on the frozen tundra. We always set the notice aside, along with other things that can and should wait, like the correspondence from American Express—at once threatening to cancel our privileges and offering us The Gold Card.

A month later, when American Express ground forces are taking up offensive positions in the shrubs, I scramble to find the Amex bill, and there with it lies the Little League registration form, due in . . . twenty minutes!

I hastily fill it out, swearing allegiance to the League and its principles, swearing that our child is not ill nor has he/she ever been ill, and swearing finally that we would never consider taking legal action against the League or its officers no matter what the degree of negligence and resultant dismemberment. If they loaded the bats with nitroglycerin at Little League headquarters, we wouldn't hold it against them.

Of course, we don't actually *read* such documents—you have to be *crazy* to do that. You'd never let your kid out of the house. And with no time to consider the ramifications, I check the little box in the lefthand corner that reads: "I Volunteer My Services to Help the League"—whatever that means.

I speed over to The Commissioner's private residence, my son falls on his icy steps, rings the doorbell, and hands the form and the personal check to a scowling Mrs. Foozle, who checks her watch, then snaps them out of his hand. Over the course of thirty years of Working With Young People,

Mrs. Foozle has apparently concluded they're detestable.

My wife marks the date for tryouts on the Master Calendar (the only critical document we own, listing birthday parties, cocktail parties, karate lessons, dental appointments, my wife's birthday, appointments for pet vaccinations and other critical dates), yet when that date in March for tryouts arrives you look out the window and you still *cannot believe* anyone in his right mind would schedule baseball tryouts when winter's not even over yet. "You sure the tryouts aren't *April* 17, dear?"

Getting out the old baseball mitts and thumping your fists into them is always referred to as a Rite of Spring. Men write tearful magazine articles for one thousand dollars about it. But it is not spring, not by a long shot—vernal (bleeping) equinox or no vernal equinox—and it sure doesn't feel rite at all, not yet.

March is a particularly ugly time of year here in the northern climes. God is trying to tell us to return to our centrally heated homes, but Commissioner Foozle dictates otherwise.

As you are out chipping ice from your windshield, The Commissioner calls to remind you that back in January you marked that little box at the bottom of your child's registration form—oh *yes* you did, lefthand corner!—stating that you would be happy to volunteer your services. "You are a coach," he said, enthusiastically. Yet somehow you feel less like you have received good news than a grim diagnosis.

The first ramification is that you can't just drop your kid off at tryouts. You have to attend the tryouts, with a clipboard, to evaluate the players.

The temperature at tryouts in the north is usually around thirty-nine degrees, with a light rain falling, *just* light enough so that tryouts will still be held. Peak discomfort.

Flocks of geese heading north for summer are making U-turns in the sky.

Cars pull into the parking lot by the baseball field, and grimacing kids in ski jackets accompanied by dour adults disembark.

They meld into the swarm of confusion cooked up by Commissioner Foozle and his band of merry men. Each new arrival asks: "What's going on?"

The answer goes something like this: Boys aged eight and nine enrolled in Washington, Jefferson and Lincoln schools are to try out here between 8:00 and 9:15 A.M., no one seems to know when girls like yours aged nine and ten enrolled in Nixon, Agnew and Quayle schools and desiring to play in the Mixed Junior Ponytail (West) League are scheduled to try out. No one.

You do not find this out, however, until the onset of hypothermia from standing in a long Zhivago-esque line of parents and kids leading to a card table.

If we're lucky, the grass will be terribly soggy and the batter's box slippery mud. If not, it will still be frozen tundra.

Despite the weather, a drive around town the day before tryouts reveals lots of dads out with their kids, in yards and on baseball diamonds, tossing the ball around—trying to teach their kids How To Play Baseball. This is a desperate exercise, of course, akin to cracking the Spanish book for the first time the night before the final exam. I know.

Now, getting out and Playing Catch With Your Child *sounds* like a swell idea—"Son, let's play catch!"—but watching these preseason games of catch, it often seems that neither parent nor child is really having a good time.

The first few flips back and forth are fine: an

errant toss here, a missed catch there—no problem. However, about a minute and fifteen seconds into the little game of catch, Dad starts making suggestions: "You have to throw it right to me, honey"; "Take a step toward me and throw the ball."

Although it's called "a game of *catch,*" Daddy's little boy or girl is not actually catching the ball all that often. And he or she doesn't really throw it hard enough, let alone in the right direction. This is crunch time. Tryouts are tomorrow. Dad grows edgy.

Fathers and sons—now fathers and daughters, too—are obligated to play catch. Boys, particularly, must play baseball, and their fathers are *responsible* for how well they play.

"Pay attention!"

"Did you hear what I said? Take a step toward me before you throw."

"You're never going to get it if you don't listen!"

"Eye on the ball!"

"Oh, so you're just giving up. That's typical."

Focus is always the problem. Kids like to fool around too much these days. They can't concentrate anymore. They're too soft. Lazy. Worthless! Too much TV! Don't have the toughness. They're not hungry. That's why Japan . . . oh never mind. Just get a little bit serious for *one minute,* willya!

In baseball as in life, it's the fundamental question: how much to push?

For parents and kids, the spring tryouts are reunions of sorts. You see people you haven't seen since last season, and—like high school reunions—there are those you are happy to see and there are those you had hoped you'd never see again in your life. There are wonderful people you may have shared triumphs and tragedies with during previous seasons; people you argued with; people the very sight of whom puts knots in your stomach; people you hoped had moved away, some to Peoria, others all the way to the happy hunting grounds.

Say! Isn't that the-guy-who-should-never-be-allowed-around-children? He's here every year! Bud Flint coaches baseball, soccer, football, basketball, lacrosse—you name it. He's there. He thinks games are basic training at Parris Island, that he is a drill instructor, and these are Marine recruits. He hasn't smiled yet. There's still time. He's only forty-two.

Shivering kids in wet down garments finally check in at the right card table, then are sent to line up over by the backstop for a half hour or more to await their turns at bat.

Sometimes even the best of them can't hit the ball after not picking up a bat for nine months. Sometimes the worst of them hits the ball by accident. Sometimes the dad pitching hits them. He hasn't thrown a ball for nine years: "Sorry, you all right?" Don't ask. It makes them cry.

Willie comes to the plate. He looks awkward and nervous. He is wearing a T-shirt, flannel shirt, wool sweater and a winter coat. The batter's box is slippery mud. He is holding a frozen bat, trying to hit pitches thrown over his head and at his ankles by a man trying to pitch in a down coat from a mound that is likewise slippery mud.

"Have you ever thought of just putting us in straitjackets?" asks one husky kid. "Smart ass," one of the coaches mumbles. Bad attitude. Not good for the program. You know what one bad apple can do.

"What's your name, kid?" I ask.

"B.A."

I think I like this kid.

They use these terrible *aluminum* bats now, of

course—supposedly for safety. Wooden bats could splinter and Poke Out Someone's Eye. Or something like that. Who knows? Ask a lobbyist for the Aluminum Council.

Meanwhile, try wrapping your fingers around a thirty-nine-degree aluminum shaft sometime. It's about as much fun as putting your tongue on an ice cube tray. And that's not the worst of it. The worst is that if you happen to actually *hit*—by some act of divine intervention—the frozen hardball with a frozen aluminum bat it's like an electroshock treatment. A kid no more wants to hit a hardball with a frozen aluminum bat than a lab rat wants to eat out of a bowl hooked up to a car battery. Few do.

I watch Willie from afar. I am on the next diamond, assigned to rate kids on catching and throwing. I see Willie whiff at six pitches and he looks upset. I do so want him to do well. Sometimes I wonder why it matters so much to me. One reason, I think, is that I look upon him as part of me, and if he succeeds, I succeed. That's the sick part. The other part is that I want him to succeed because I know it will make him happy. I want him to be happy. I recall how disappointing baseball really is so much of the time. If you're terrific you get a hit three times out of ten. It's why so many kids segue into track, tennis, lacrosse. It's embarrassing to stand up there alone, in front of everybody, and fail. Fail in football, and nobody knows if it's your fault or the ten other guys. In baseball it's you and you alone, striking out.

My basic position with Willie is: I don't ever want him to fail; I don't ever want him to know disappointment; to feel pain, to feel hurt of any kind. Is that so unrealistic?

Finally Willie does—Plink!—one out to shallow center field and the man pitching tells him "that's enough." Willie is not happy with hitting one ball out of seven. That is an understatement. "Everyone's rusty," I tell him. And even though that's almost true, he is not consoled. He doesn't need a pep talk. He needs bereavement counseling.

It doesn't help, of course, that standing next to the pitcher is this guy, this ominous presence, with a clipboard. He is rating the batters' performance on a scale of one to five. The man is none other than Dick Knavery, one of those perennial coaches who always offers to "help out" at the tryouts. In this way they spot the best players and control the ratings. Dick has been known to underrate some of the very best players so they will be overlooked in the draft and he can get them on his team.

A draft in Little League? Oh yes. Chicanery, at this level? Of the highest order.

We don't like Dick.

Dick has also been known to tell certain talented players—ones he'd like to get in the draft—that they don't have to show up for tryouts. If the other coaches don't even know about the kid, they won't pick him. He has no rating; isn't even on the list. Knavery picks him.

Knavery's kid, Richard Junior, whom the other kids refer to as "Little Dick," comes to bat and swings wildly at three pitches, missing them all by a foot. He looks terrible. What other coaches looking on may not realize is that Little Dickie is *trying* to look bad.

You see, coaches automatically get their own kid in the draft—although in the next town "a manager may waive the option on his son" (Section XII-i-1). Wow.

The Commissioner decides in which round you must take your own child. If he does well in tryouts you have to take him in, say, the first or second round, when you'd rather be picking other good players. If he doesn't do so well in tryouts, you can pick him in, say, the third or fourth round—which allows you to take two good players in the first and second rounds. Get it? Dick does.

Hate that guy. Don't want to be like him. And yet: I don't want *him* beating *me*! My team, that is. Standing over there with a smug look on his face, thinking he's a better coach, better person.

Some coaches are at the opposite end of the spectrum. Sloppy guys who live in ramshackle houses with kids who get C-pluses in school and who own big, smelly dogs. Guys like Norb Lookingbill.

He doesn't even show up for the tryouts and evaluations, trusting the ratings that Knavery will present to him at the draft. Like a Pekingese wandering into a pit bull ring, Lookingbill and his ilk will be losers—at least in the won-lost column.

Last year, coaching my daughters softball team, I was asked to help out with evaluations. (Yes, I too wanted to be there to scout the talent; I'm a lot closer to the Knavery end of the spectrum than I like to admit.)

The league director, a mellow sort, told me to

evaluate the pitchers. In girl's softball, as in boy's baseball, pitching is the most important element of the game. As I was getting set to rate the pitchers, one of the other coaches ran over and stopped the proceedings: "Oh no! I handle the pitchers." I conceded and went out to evaluate catching and throwing. Later, all would agree that the pitchers' evaluations were bizarre. None of the great pitchers seemed to have high scores. Hmm. Meanwhile, the top-*rated* pitcher was taken first in the draft by a coach who quickly discovered the girl couldn't pitch at all. "You always think you're being paranoid," said the coach who drafted her, "but, it's funny: in Little League, you never are."

I watched my daughter, Libby, swing wildly during her batting evaluation. Never hit a ball. Yet she received the highest rating. What's going on here?

I remember now.

After his audition at the plate, Willie was sent to the outfield, for his catching and throwing evaluation. Conditions were less than ideal for these activities, too, seeing that the kids were wearing mittens and gloves, and the ball was wet and slippery.

At that first tryout, you begin to glimpse how your child fits into the order of things. He drops the ball sometimes and throws wildly at others. Not pretty. But! You see kids who cannot catch the ball at all. Maybe Willie is actually good! Then you see a strong, confident kid throwing and catching as well as—better than?—your child and you wonder how many of *these* guys are around. You see his testosterone-charged father come up and command him—in so many words—to improve or else!

And you get a sinking feeling that your son may never be among the best because there are simply things you will not do. There are fathers out there who psychologically, emotionally and physically horsewhip their boys to make them the best baseball players they can possibly be. (And, after nine years I can tell you that often it works.)

Maybe there's another way! Maybe with *positive* reinforcement. . . Nah!

Willie runs over with his scorecard. He has scored a four out of a possible five in each of the three categories.

Those in charge make a terrible blunder by giving the slips of paper with the ratings on them back to the kids to turn in at the card table, rather than keeping the individual scores secret on the judges' clipboards. So the kids know when they've received terrible scores, and inevitably the kids compare.

"Ben got all fives, Daddy," Willie says. "It's so unfair. He stinks." One girl has all ones. Two other girls are laughing at her. She begins to cry.

What the kids don't realize about their ratings is that in our league, it doesn't really matter how well they do in tryouts. They all make a team. In fact, the worse they do on tryout day, the lower they'll be taken in the draft, the more good players they'll have on their team, and the better their team will be.

When I tried out for Little League, it was quite different: Life and Death. If you didn't do well, you were put on a farm league team in the minors with nerds, spazzes, geeks and retards, which strongly suggested to you that quite possibly you too were a nerd, a spaz, a geek or a retard.

As Willie and the others compare scores, I notice that some judges gave number ones for the best performances, while other judges gave number fives for the best.

The entire exercise was meaningless.

THE DRAFT

Wow! Jack was playing hardball!

Jack Caper made the first pick in the Little League draft and Commissioner Barney Foozle repeated it dramatically for the other coaches seated in his—wood?—paneled family room.

"Jack Caper selects . . . number sixty-six, Joey Dominico . . . the first player in the first round. Joey Dominico."

Huh? Whaaa? This set the other coaches to scratching their heads, blurting out "Who? What's-his-name?" and riffling through their player evaluation sheets. They didn't have anybody by any such name down as any sort of standout. Who *was* this guy?

I knew. Joey wasn't the standout. But his

mother, Angela, certainly *was*—one of the few . . . mothers . . . to have ever worn spike heels and a skin-tight gold lamé bodysuit to a Little League competition. Angela always looked like she was dressed to attend a prize fight in Atlantic City.

Those infamous chartreuse short-shorts weren't bad either (Little League Hall of Fame, perhaps?), which she wore so well in tandem with a scanty top that didn't reach anywhere near the top of the shorts—in part because of her 1991 breast implants. She had a stomach that flattened out moments after childbirth, she looked young enough to be Joey's sister and was consequently widely despised by other mothers in Ridgewood. Veteran scorekeepers have been known to fall several innings behind with Angela in the stands.

Jack Caper was implementing his own unique strategy for drafting a Little League team: "I choose the kids with the best-looking mothers," he explains.

This is something I flatly refused to do—at least until the later rounds. I had too many holes to fill on my squad. I like to win, plus: I needed a kid with a pool. A swimming pool. For the postseason party. That's my philosophy.

There are many approaches. Some coaches

keep dossiers on practically every kid in town in their computers. Others make a point of drafting kids with older brothers; the younger sibling always seems to have picked up a lot from the older brother.

Coach Lefty Mano always went after a kid whose parents were recent immigrants, didn't understand the customs of our country, and gave, like, *Rolex watches* as coaches' gifts at the end of the season. Conehead Syndrome, I called it. One year such a family gave dollar bills to Trick or Treaters. Kids were changing masks and coming back.

But for the most part the draft is very serious business. "Nothing we say leaves this room," Barney would sometimes say, ominously, to open the proceedings.

There is always a veneer of congeniality as the coaches arrive. But this melts away quickly as the eight coaches draw numbers out of a hat to determine the order of selection. Number one drafts first in the first round, but in the second round eight drafts first. Always. Except the year I sent my wife to the basketball draft in my stead. The men were all terribly congenial—"more French onion dip, my dear?"—but told her that, having drawn number eight, she would select last in every round. We struggled that season.

The Commisioner, Barney Foozle, talks tenderly and caringly—and at once, absolutely *mindlessly*—about children. He is given to doing things like ordering five hundred hats all the same color for the league, when he's supposed to order different colors for the different teams.

Barney gave his little speech about the idea of the draft being to come up with eight equal teams, because Winning Is Not Important, before the eight coaches set about selecting their teams in a wild flurry of rascality.

Before the selecting began, Bud Flint, an old hand at these drafts, whipped out a letter stating that the parents of the best overall player at the tryouts—a kid named "Smash" Danner, with straight five-pluses in the ratings—desired nothing more in life than to have their son have an opportunity to be coached by Buddy Flint, because of Buddy's Strong Personal Relationship with the boy and because of Buddy's Record of Service to the Community.

Predictably, Foozle thought this was wonderful, that a boy and a coach would have such a close personal relationship. But Knavery was all over

Foozle and Flint, identifying this—correctly—as an obvious attempt to subvert the draft process.

No one questioned Knavery's expertise in this area.

Other coaches pleaded that so and so "is best friends with my son" and it would be good for the two of them if they played on the same team. A coach described another boy as having emotional problems and said, "I am like a second father to him."

Then Knavery brought out The List. His list of co-coaches. Probably the greatest scam going in Little League baseball is the old Co-Coach Trick. It can decide the outcome of a season before the draft is even held, much less before any baseball is played.

It always reminds me of my days as a reporter and occasional poll watcher in Chicago during the reign of Richard J. Daley, when elections were determined before the polls even opened. The voting machines would be delivered to the polling places with hundreds of votes already registered for Daley's Democratic candidates.

Dick Daley had nothing on Dick Knavery. Knavery presented his list of six—count 'em—co-coaches, who all happened to be the fathers (plus one mother) of good baseball players. A coach is not only entitled to his own child in the draft, but also to the children of each co-coach.

"How can you have six?" I objected. "What's Mr. Huffman (father of "Mean Gene" Huffman, the best pitcher in town)? Your strength and fitness coach? Motivational specialist? Team nutritionist? What?"

As Mr. Huffman tells it, Knavery called him up the previous September—September!—and asked if he'd like to coach with him next season. This was after Mean Gene registered eight wins and no losses as a pitcher and hit a home run every third trip to the plate. Mr. Huffman informed Knavery that he knew nothing about baseball, but Knavery assured him that didn't matter, adding: "We need a good man to keep the scorebook."

Knavery *and* Flint sent the Huffmans Christmas cards and Knavery invited them over for dinner, where Knavery and his wife, Bev, worked as a tag team. It is said that at the appropriate moment one evening at a dinner party, after dessert and many aperitifs, in flickering candlelight, Bev looked into the eyes of Steve, father of an all-star pitcher, and breathed: "Oh Steve, we simply must be together . . . next season."

So, Knavery's first seven men (counting his own son) in the batting order were taken care of—all seven among the best at the tryouts. So, first place had pretty well been determined, before the draft began.

Jack Caper selected Joey Dominico's mother and the draft itself was under way.

Knavery selected Mean Gene, and I was next. I had to select my son, whom Barney decided was an obvious first-round selection after hearing testimony from the other coaches.

It's a crazy thing to watch. The other coaches all say that your son is among the best ballplayers ever to play the game—even if he's a complete spaz. They say this so you'll have to take him in the first round.

You retort that your son is not so hot, pretty bad actually, abominable! A disgrace to the family. A bad baseball player, yes, but that's only the half of it! A constant troublemaker, a bad kid all the way around, a head case. Not to mention: he is scheduled for arm surgery in the morning! Surgeons say they may have to take the arm, the right arm, his *throwing* arm, gentlemen!

But it doesn't matter what you say. They made me take my daughter in the first round of the basketball draft last year even though she scored four points the entire previous season!

Tony Dragonetti was next and selected a kid no one had ever heard of. It turned out to be a new kid in town no one knew about. Tony had seen him play baseball—a killer!—and told him to lie low and not to come to tryouts. No one gave Tony a hard time about this, or anything else for that matter. Tony owns a modest twelve-washer, three-dryer Laundromat and lives in a $2.7 million home. Really knows how to stretch a dollar.

Lefty had to take his kid in the first round, too. His son was good and Lefty was a good coach. He was my nemesis, but a friendly, good-natured one, who played by the book and took his kid to the In The Swing batting cages to hit one thousand balls a week. That's a hundred-dollar-a-week habit, plus he has Roy White, ex-big leaguer, coach his kid in private batting lessons at fifty dollars a half hour. So he spends several thousand dollars a year making his kid a better hitter. Yelling at him a lot about his hitting really seems to help too.

Although Smash Danner was still available, Norb Lookingbill, the mope amongst us, picked some kid no one had ever heard of. We were all for that. Norbert was totally out of it. Hadn't a clue. Went around saying things like "It's only a game" and "They're just kids"—things that made no sense to us. "Do we have to draft? Just give me a team," he'd say. His players last year called him "Yo, Norb."

Like so many dweebs, he coached a lot. He coached my daughter's soccer team, despite not really knowing *exactly* how many players are on a soccer team, let alone the names of the positions. He also seemed to have a little trouble remembering *precise* times and places of games and practices. "Yo, Norb."

And so it was that in the first round, Yo Norb selected Michelle Flint, one of the premier flautists in town. "Nice girl," Lefty remarked, in the way my college roommate used to say "terrific personality" when he was fixing me up with a blind date.

And, yes, Michelle *is* related to Coach Buddy Flint. Daughter. But it seems Buddy had waived the right to draft his daughter—at her request.

No matter how perfect the system of tryouts, evaluations and drafting procedures, Little League teams will never be equal so long as there are Yo

Norbs coaching against the likes of a Dick Knavery, who keeps the names and evaluations of every child he can think of—hundreds!—in his computer: name, age, how well they field, hit and throw, and whether they have been on any all-star teams. Yes!

Coach Bill Shoulders was next and he snapped up Smash Danner, causing Buddy Flint, who had next pick, to throw his pen clear across the family room. Flint had noticed that the coveted Smash had not been selected yet, and he was holding his breath and praying—some said you could see his lips moving!—that he could still get him.

Flint selected a terrible ballplayer, but "a hard-nosed kid with a good work ethic." That was Buddy's brand of player. Buddy seemed perpetually pissed off because his philosophy of life and baseball didn't win out as often as he thought it should. He knew he was right to take "hard-working, coachable" kids, but he was so impressed with that single quality that he was blind to the fact that his picks were often supremely untalented.

Something of a disappointment in life—at work and home—Flint's life had become Little League. He was coming off a one-year suspension for punching another coach. He was not suspended for life because of his "Commitment to Youth."

Seems he goes around giving totally inappropriate "Just Say No" lectures designed for eighteen-year-old ghetto kids to first graders in this upper-middle-class suburb. (Seems to me that any faintly rebellious kid would be encouraged to try drugs once Bud Flint told him not to.)

Flint would pass on good players he had deemed "head cases" or "troublemakers." The Uncoachables. They're branded at an early age, even though some of them have far more talent, and a lot more spirit, than the compliant "coachables." But if it's good enough for our school system, it's good enough for Little League baseball.

I've won any number of league championships taking head cases and troublemakers. I tried a couple more in this draft: B.A., whose parents were strongly considering military school (in Germany, I believe) for their ten-year-old, and Andy, who at ten years old sometimes came to see Willie at 11:30 P.M. His goal in life? To eat everything on the McDonald's menu at one sitting. "They keep *adding* things," he complained, "like salads. Can't gag a salad." Heavy hitter. Caper passed him up because his mother had put on about forty pounds in the off-season, and Caper said he couldn't afford to take Andy to the ice cream parlor after a team victory. "Triple scoop with sprinkles, every time," Caper warned.

Speaking of fat chances, coaches are actually supposed to *help* each other in the draft so that the teams are balanced. "Anybody know this Kossick kid?" Tony asked at a basketball draft. If anybody knew anything, he was supposed to speak up. Nobody said much of anything, except: "No, no, can't say as I do." I was biting the back of my hand. Mark Kossick was a new arrival, one of the three best players in town and I had the next pick after Tony! "He's supposed to be good!" said the basketball Commissioner. I glared at the Commissioner and finished second that year. Tony picked Mark Kossick and—through no fault of his own—finished first.

If a kid is good, nobody says much. If a kid is not good, you might say, "I heard that he was pretty good. . ." adding, after the other coach takes him, ". . . before the accident." Heh-heh.

I've made suggestions for changing this draft system, which gets the coaches' egos too heavily involved, and . . . Doesn't Work. It never produces balanced teams. It would work as well to just put all the kids' names in a bowl and fish them out at random.

Last season I proposed another system. I called the league director and proposed that, using the accumulated knowledge of all the coaches—to include all that's stored in Knavery's computer—we all sit down together and try to assemble eight balanced teams. *Then* randomly assign a coach to each team.

I think this must have sounded vaguely . . . un-American . . . or something to The Commissioner, who stammered and said it was "too late" to revise the system (even though tryouts had not been held!), and who informed me that he had never seen a year yet when a team didn't win at least one-third of its games!

"You'll never change things," another coach opined. "These guys have spent years figuring out how to rig the system and getting themselves into the positions to do it."

I don't know about *that,* but I do know that we did things the old way last year, and the team I co-coached finished in first place, and another team didn't win one single game. And I still think they ought to change things.

♦ ♦ ♦

The day after the draft, a father whose name was on Flint's list of co-coaches (oh yes, he also had a list) called my house. I wasn't home. He informed my wife that his son did not want to be on Flint's team under any circumstances, that his son had been on Flint's basketball team, didn't like him and wanted to be on my team.

My wife told him she'd have to call The Commissioner's Office.

Foozle was bamboozled. "But you were on his list of co-coaches."

"Whaaat?!"

"He said you wanted to coach with him."

"No!"

Another Commissioner might have said: "Aha!" and launched an investigation. Foozle was perplexed. He put his son, Charlie, on my team. I was happy about this, of course, because to have a player who was actually born to one of Flint's co-coaches was almost too good to be true. A player with papers!

But at a price. Barb Flint launched a campaign accusing my co-coach, Gerald Meeks (Hermie's dad), and me of conspiring to snatch Charlie away from Flint's team. Mrs. Flint said Gerald had fostered the idea among the boys that they could change teams if they wanted to. Gerald denied having done this and countered that surely this was the pot calling the kettle black; that it was, after all, Flint himself who had subverted the process by bringing in his list of coaches and falsely claiming that Charlie's father wanted to coach. It was the talk of Agnew Elementary.

Meanwhile, I knew nothing of this. We were having a party, my wife had invited the Flints—Why?!—and Barb called to say that they "could not consider attending under these conditions!"

What conditions? I asked, and for two hours she enumerated them. Barb and others associated with Flint's team—including people who are supposed to be some of my best friends!—had embroidered the story by saying that my son had been going around telling the other kids at school that Flint was a cheater and that his son had heard these remarks and was "emotionally disturbed."

I drove to school, pulled my son out of class and told him not to say things like that about Mr. Flint ("Although true," I wanted to add). As it turned out, Barb's son testified to her that it was not my son saying those things.

At the Teacher Appreciation Dance that weekend, the imbroglio was all anyone talked about. Two years later, Gerald's son is still not invited to Barb's son's parties. Relationships are icy all the way around. Barb is still not speaking to Gerald, who says "I couldn't care less." But he says it every day.

If you are a Little League coach, even while you sit in your living room reading the paper and minding your own business—This Could Happen to You!

WHY WE COACH

1. It's something Bill Cosby would do.
2. What the heck, we go to all the games anyway.
3. We think it will be fun.
4. We think that we might be, probably would be, pretty darned good at it.
5. Your kid's coach last year was an idiot. He knew nothing about baseball and—luckily, I suppose—couldn't communicate with children.
6. The coach who wears a "Kill 'Em All and Let God Sort 'Em Out" T-shirt called to say he'd love to have your child on his team this year.
7. It's really the *only* way to insure the grotesquely preferential treatment you want for your child.
8. Hey, how bad could it be?

Dateline: Willow Springs, Illinois, August 8, 1990—John Hills, coach of his son's youth baseball team, was listed in stable condition in the intensive care unit at LaGrange Memorial Hospital today, after being treated for fractured ribs, a broken nose and severe bruises received when he was beaten by a rival coach and players.

The rival coach, George Loy, of Bridgeview, was handcuffed by Willow Springs police and charged with two counts of battery. A Bridgeview player was charged in a juvenile petition with striking Hills with a bat.

The two coaches had argued the calls of umpires during the game. Hills was attacked after uttering the phrase: "It's only a game." His team had just taken the lead.

Coaches don't like each other much. From the moment they see other coaches at the tryouts, holding their clipboards, the juices begin to flow—bile for the most part. You know that winning—or so they *say*—is not what Little League is all about . . . and yet . . . *you want to beat that . . . that prick . . . Knavery.* The children on his team may be just as nice as they can be, but he has become the enemy. You want to bury the cretin. He takes the game too seriously. Not like me. Hate that guy.

Many coaches come to believe—despite what they say to the contrary—that this isn't really a game between kids at all, but a game between them, a game of who teaches best, who motivates best, whose strategy is the best, who's smarter.

It's all many of the coaches really have. If they are stifled at work and at home, it becomes their only real domain to prove their worth.

Coaching kids can become their lives. They ease into it, but soon are having shirts made up with the inscription "Ridgewood Baseball" and attending weekly meetings year round. They say that they are "doing it for the kids," and you know what? A few of them are.

They may take over the game completely and guard it zealously against outsiders. In a nearby town, Selden, New York, the Little League board of directors refused to hold open meetings and would not conduct annual elections. When they were pressured into holding elections and a new board was voted in, the old board locked up all the equipment and started a rival league, laying claim to all of the ballfields. The matter went to court.

To coach or not to coach?

Probably not. I've done it, fulfilled my civic obligation. I'm not really an *expert* on the game; I don't have enough time to really do the job properly; the parents are always a big pain.

And yet! You come to realize that if *you* don't do it some . . . *twit* . . . will. This twit will actually know less than you do; he will not know how to relate to children, he will lose every game and your child will cry. Moreover, he may not even let your child play! You don't want to be unfair about this in any way, but if you volunteer your time to coach, doesn't your kid *deserve* the edge? Coach think.

Now you may think when you check that little box on the application form that this means you will be considered for a possible coaching position, that perhaps you will start out as one of the assistant coaches, that you will merely be *involved* in coaching. This is true, but in much the same way that you are merely *involved* in, say, an airplane crash.

You check the box, you get a team—and beg for help.

Almost immediately, little thoughts begin creeping into your head. You *know* that winning is not a *goal* of Little League baseball—Certainly Not!—nor is it *your* goal. But! Maybe, just maybe, you should call B.A.'s parents to see if they'd like to just Help Out With The Team. You know, just get out there and Have a Little Fun—as a co-coach.

His parents come to mind because they are Nice People, Decent People, Good People, God-fearing People (one would think), who share your sense of values, and who have raised a lovely child who can, as it happens, Hit the Ball Into the F——ing TREES!

I know about this because I myself am courted before basketball season for my tall son and my tall daughter. Guys who crawl sideways on trees and suck moss call and want, suddenly, to be best friends.

You are starting down that long road to going nuts by season's end.

Coaches come in a wide variety of types.

There is The Innocent, who actually *believes* that this is all just Good Clean Fun. These coaches can be fine, but the largest substratum under The

Innocent seems to be those known to the kids as "Mopes." Take Yo Norb, for example.

Casual empirical evidence suggests to me that the most prevalent type of coach is probably someone just shy of the Win-At-All-Costs egomaniac, the aforementioned chess player, using the kids as pawns. If your guess for what the kids might call this type of coach is "butthead," you have selected the right answer.

Take Dick Knavery. For him the Little League diamond is a proving ground. He is trying to change the game from one based on the skills of preadolescents to one based on adult strategy. Because he wins a lot, he is often portrayed as a brute, who argues every call, illegally stacks his team and violates rules in order to win.

And he may not even be the worst! The worst is probably Moral Man, a coach like Bud Flint, a Character Builder, who sees nothing fun about the game. I don't even think he'd like me using the word "game."

To him the Little League field of *play* (sorry again, Bud) is a place for children to learn Life's Lessons, Hard Truths, the value of Hard Work, and other Traditional Wholesome Family Values. To him, winning is not only good, it is virtuous. Losing, he attributes to moral failure: "You were scared out there," "You gave up on me." Willie had a basketball coach like that when he was fourteen, a coach who got mad at him and his teammates for allowing themselves to be "intimidated" by a team of kids two and three years older than they were in a Sunday-morning league in Harlem. That team was the Gauchos, said to be one of the best youth teams in the nation. It's not always moral failure, coach, sometimes the other team is just . . . a lot better. Get it?

Flint sees Little League baseball as a distinctly moral endeavor, training boys to be Upstanding Citizens—in the model of the Boy Scouts and other adult-directed, youth-oriented programs. This may be why I didn't much care for the Boy Scouts either. On a nice day when we should have been playing sandlot baseball (with NO adult supervision), we were always at some Scout meeting with a guy like Yo Norb or Flint commanding us to staple a variety of knots to a piece of plywood.

Flint calls the kids "youngsters"—to their faces! He, too, is often referred to by the kids as "that butthead"—a term that as you can see has broad application in the Little League community.

Flint is given to using the figure "a hundred and

ten percent" a lot, the word "Hustle!" and phrases like: "Wipe that smile off your face, mister!" He's a little angry all the time, probably because corporal punishment is not encouraged in the league. George Patton and to a lesser degree Norman Schwarzkopf are his heroes. Of course those men are not commanding ten-year-olds, but Moral Man works with what he's got.

Sometimes Flint will lose it during a game, and yell, "Get that little bastard," or "This batter stinks," or some other inappropriate remark that the rest of us only dare mutter.

A coach must walk a thin line to keep from being perceived as . . . overinvolved.

"I'm so disgusted with you guys, I'm gonna go sit in the stands!" Bud will say. "I'm embarrassed to be on the same bench with you. You're smelling up the place!"

Ah! But underinvolved—"overdistancing," as they called it in the coaches' seminar—is perceived as being just as bad, leading to chaos, and what's worse: Losing.

Coaches like Yo Norb who say it doesn't matter if they win or lose are often viewed as "wimps"—and believe me it does matter to the kids if they win or lose. They like to win.

Jack Caper also says it doesn't matter, yet he's not viewed as a wimp. He teaches his kids baseball, but doesn't froth at the mouth at the draft or during games. I guess Jack would be the ideal. And yet—parents complain because his teams don't win enough.

The only thing about being one of the underinvolved is that there's a tremendous feeling of righteousness when Bud Flint goes crazy and we have to call the animal warden. When he loses control, everybody throws up their hands and says: "See? Told you he was a butthead."

No one really knows how to coach properly, and times being what they are, many coaches turn to clinics, seminars, books and home videos on the subject.

At the little local clinics they always emphasize that it's All For Fun, Only A Game, Winning Is Not The Most Important Thing.

So, the kids might ask: why *do* the best players play the most important positions? Why *does* our coach jump up and down when we win, and call the other coach the A-word when we lose? And get mad when I strike out? Why do our parents scream so and call the umpire names? Everybody certainly *acts* as though winning were important!

There are more professional approaches to coaching offered at area-wide seminars with titles like "Little League Psychology." Of course, the guys who need it most don't go. I did, once.

"Some kids need a pat on the head, others need a kick in the butt," said Dale Kopf, a veteran Little League coach, who said at the seminar that he was accustomed to the customary coaching duties of baby-sitter, teacher, manager, chauffeur and disciplinarian—but found that this was not enough, he had to be a child psychologist as well.

One of the coaches described it as "a workshop to cut down on the hollering and screaming," others said it was to make coaches become "more in touch with their players' emotions," "more sensitive to their fears and frailties."

There were helpful hints given, such as having kids run around the bases backward or doing the duck walk or hopping like bunnies if they became bored. My kids would quit! Or report me to The Commissioner's Office.

I can hear Geraldo now: "Geist told the children he wanted to become more "in touch' with them, more 'sensitive' to them—then made the children run around the bases backward in the heat and humiliated them by making them do a duck walk. The man is sick!"

A league director from another town was so taken with the whole spirit of the seminar that he went home and suggested not keeping score in the games with six-year-olds. Parents shouted him down.

All of this is an attempt to haul coaches out of the Neanderthal age of preadolescent relations.

Some are too basic. In one coaching symposium, social behaviorists specializing in small-group cultures began with stuff like "Try to Refrain from Pistol Whipping the Children"—or something like that. (This is where they lost credibility with coaches Bill Shoulders and Bud Flint.)

In others they try to turn volunteer Little League coaches into practicing child psychologists, talking about: "Our Male Dominated Culture" or "Sex-Role Development in the Preadolescent Male" and exploring the fact that "most nonfamilial guardians of boys are women." I think they mean teachers.

They talk of baseball's "symbolic centrality in our culture," while Shoulders and Flint just shake their heads, shrug their shoulders and vow not to return after the lunch break. What the . . . ? They thought this thing was going to be about squeeze bunts, hook slides and the sacrifice fly.

They talk about coaches having didactic roles, teaching baseball and values. Bud Flint always perks up during this portion of the seminar, even though he has no idea what *didactic* means.

From these seminars I find that my own approach is interactionist ("Keep your butt down when fielding a ball"), my focus analytic, not ameliorative. That's what they tell me. Should I be seeing somebody about this?

"Coaches should keep their players orderly and oriented to the serious performance of baseball, while displaying emotional coolness." I wrote that one down.

In addition to holding a degree in psychology, it is also beneficial to have a couple of years of med school under your belt. Your specialty? Cold Paks. Artificial ice. Use it for everything. I don't want to say that the country is drifting into hypochondria . . . but, anyway, in Little League, everything is treated as an injury—and ice applied. Sympathy, while *thought* to be good, may actually exacerbate the situation. Players may not even be considering crying until you put your arm around them and ask if it hurts.

At the other end of the spectrum, however, when someone on Flint's or Shoulders's team breaks a leg, these two guys tell the kid to "Walk it off."

The volunteer coach can also turn to the library or bookstore for help but probably won't get it.

Little League's Official How-to-Play-Baseball Book is typically off the mark, bearing no relationship to reality.

After a chapter on warming-up exercises, which almost no one in Little League ever does, the first matter addressed is "Gripping the Ball": "You should grip the ball exactly the same way every time you throw it," the book says.

"Put your index and middle fingers across the wide seams, and hold the ball with the inside edge of your thumb on the opposite side. There should be a space between your index and middle fingers about the width of your index finger. Your ring finger and pinkie should rest on the side of the ball. Wrap your index and middle fingers over the top of the ball, holding it with equal, even pressure from the base of your fingers to the tips. You should be able to see a space between the palm of your hand and the ball. Even if your hands are small you should be able to make that space. Don't try to crush the ball. Keep your hand relaxed. You should use this grip every time you throw the ball."

Whaaat?! By the time you do all of these things, the guy who hit the ball will have rounded the bases and repaired to the ice cream parlor for an evening of celebration. Might be old enough to have a drink.

All my Little League coach said was: "Hey! You! Stop throwing like a girl!"

"You should grip the ball exactly the same way every time you throw it"?!

There is a companion video, too, in which Coach Saul and Coach Ron give you the same advice.

The book says: "Don't choke up." Are they kidding? Little League coaches would love to have a nickel for every time a kid got a hit after being told to "Choke Up!" but, alas, there are not enough nickels in circulation.

Well, so much for self-help.

In addition to the merely unhelpful books, there are those that are actually a little frightening.

I picked up one entitled *Youth League Baseball* that scared me to death. It stated that Little League baseball is "a serious enterprise, as is going to school or to church." Whoa!

You quickly realize that most of those writing these books are control freaks, heavily into emotional bondage, with an anal compulsive bent, coaching for their own ego fulfillment. The book speaks much of "discipline and teamwork and sweat," regarding the sport as essentially no fun at all.

"My team," states the author, "will be neat and clean for games, with shirts tucked in and the uniform worn properly." Reminds me of the army. That is not good.

"The basic objective (!) of youth baseball," the book states, "is to help build character—courage, temperance, fairness and knowledge." And the author goes on to quote biblical proverbs.

I gave this book to Flint. He *loved* it. I mean instead of demanding 110 percent from his team, the way Flint does, the author of this book demands "125 percent"! Awesome.

♦ ♦ ♦

This is a glossary of jargon used on Little League diamonds worldwide. Much of it is meaningless. That is not a concern. It will help you sound like a veteran who knows what he's talking about even though you don't.

—Little chatter out there!
  —Hey-batta-batta-batta.
  —Hustle!
  —Be ready!
  —Good-Eye!
  —Eye on the ball.
  —You closed your eyes.
  —Swing if it's good.
  —(But) Make it be your pitch.
  —Walk's as good as a hit.
  —That was over your head!
  —You need a golf club to hit that!
  —Run!
  —Don't run!
  —Run on anything!
  —Choke up!
  —Wake up!

—Stand up!
—The game's over here!
—Put your glove on!
—Other hand!
—I said: put on the catcher's equipment!
—Now!
—Don't argue.
—I'll get you in the infield as soon as I can.
—Isn't it too dark for their team to bat?
—Looked good from here, ump.
—Don't be afraid of the ball.
—Can you move your fingers?
—Rub it.
—Walk it off.
—Put some ice on it.
—Throw the ball!
—Don't throw your bat.
—We gotta play them one game at a time.
—You're asleep out there.
—I need a hundred and ten percent.
—(To the opposing coach) If that's the way you want to win . . .
—What did you call me?
—Pull the trigger, Tony baby (even if no one is named Tony, it somehow sounds more impressive this way).

—Little Bingo.
—One time.
—You little s——(muttered, alone or as an addendum to any of the above).
—OK, twenty-six runs and we're right back in this thing.

FIRST PRACTICE—RAINED OUT

SECOND PRACTICE—RAINED OUT

THIRD (AND ONLY) PRACTICE

Which brings us to our first, last and only practice before the season begins!

You don't like to see a lot of sarongs and saris when you drive up to your first practice. I saw several. But luckily all belonged to Anand's entourage.

Two hours to teach kids how to play baseball before the season begins. Again, too cold, too wet, too early in the year for baseball north of the Mason Dixon line, but here it is: the first day of practice—a day all Little League coaches approach with hope and trepidation.

Was Andy serious about not liking sports? Maybe I can bring him around. His brother's great. Gotta have some talent somewhere. Oh, I see, there he is now. Four foot six inches tall, 115 pounds, devouring a Hershey's bar, still warm from his back pocket.

How bad will Anandy, or Anand or whatever his name is, really be? Neville? Byron "Bad Ass" McCarthy is supposed to be really good. Can he save the team? He and Charlie and Willie. Will some of the girls be able to hold their own?

Just how good are those top draft picks? Overrated? Did they have the day of their lives at tryouts? And just how bad are those last choices? There are always a few surprises both ways. Good kids who were overlooked or who somehow became coordinated since last year—blessed by the wand of the hand-eye coordination fairy. And you always wait to see: which kid will be the big pain in the ass? There's always one. And there's always one parent too.

Here she is now: "You know, Jean had a very traumatic baseball experience last year," said her mother, pulling me aside. "We felt strongly that she was being discriminated against, and her father did file a $1.7 million suit against the coach and the league."

"Jean!" I shout. "Second base. OK? No? Prefer first? No problem."

"Neville! You're (the mayor's son), you're my (frigging) shortstop.

"B.A., pitcher.

"Willie, first base. Oh, yeah. Jean's there. OK. Take third.

"Charlie! Second.

"Andy! (You're wide and slow.) You're our catcher!

"The rest of you in the outfield!"

"Oh, noooo!" they cry. When the wailing of the outfielders begins, another season is nigh.

"Just for right now," I said, trying to quell the revolt with prevarication. Hey, it works at Senate confirmation hearings.

You wonder about the kids. They wonder about you. Just like they do about a new teacher. Just how mean will this guy be? How unfair? What are the outer limits of unfairness? Will he stretch them?

Foul weather. No one wants to be here. Daylight Saving Time hasn't begun yet. Practice begins at four. Try getting home from work at 4:00 P.M. on a weeknight. Are we supposed to, like,

Quit Our Jobs for Little League? Why does practice begin at four? Because it's dark by six.

"Anand? You'll need a baseball mitt."

"Mitt?" asks the woman with him. "I am Anand's mother. I am Pritti."

Maybe, but not my type.

"Mitten?" she says.

"No, a glove. A baseball glove."

"I am sorry," she says. "I do not know this . . . glove?"

"Take a look at the ones the other kids are wearing."

Only a couple of them had even a remote idea of how to play the game, but most had on at least one hundred dollars—and in some cases two hundred dollars—worth of equipment. Very American.

Kids today show up for Little League dressed to start for the New York Yankees. Hundred-dollar gloves. Seventy-dollar bats. "Comes with a guarantee you'll hit .300," cracks the salesman. You don't have to practice or even show up for the game. The bat will do it for you, while you're home watching MTV.

Batting gloves, wristbands, flip-down sunglasses, forearm bands—*got* to have forearm bands!—baseball shoes and shin guards. Sure.

My brother was very big on mitt care. He oiled it—neat's-foot oil? What is a neat and why are their feet so inordinately oily?—night after night, like a soldier caring for his rifle. Come to think of it, he oiled his .22 rifle by the hour too, so both would be ready when push came to shove.

Willie's first glove was a good one, my daughter inherited it, and his second glove too—the big one, because she also plays first base. I like my first basemen to wear gloves similar to the nets used on commercial fishing vessels. The glove is supple like my brother's but more from years of wear, from Willie chewing on it nervously and from taking throws from Big Dave Reynolds. "Dad, come over here and listen. You can hear his throws coming!" You could, too.

My first glove was tiny and totally inflexible, like those a lot of kids have, made from some sort of miracle plastic, and about as flexible as a boat hull.

A lot of nerdy kids show up with these brand-new mitts from K-Mart, way too small and incapable of opening far enough to catch anything. What chance do these children have? They don't have a brother or a parent sharp enough to tell them what to buy.

About two games into the season Anand finally showed up with a glove, one of the plastic variety. He'd have been better off bare-handed.

You throw most of the kids out in the field at that first practice and pitch to a few others. "I hope," says Hermie, "that this does not mean I'm going to be in the outfield the whole year, or I'm quitting right now."

"Talk to your agent, Hermie," I reply nurturingly. "You won't have to play the outfield all the time."

It's cold. They all strike out. It looks like it's going to be a long, long season. Maybe Monique will quit. I hope so. Doesn't look like she's having much fun. I want to tell her: "It isn't a whole lot of fun when you're noooo good, is it?! Is it!?" But that would be wrong.

"Hold the bat with *both* hands, Monique. That's right."

Several of the kids are really terrible. Look like they won't hit or catch a ball all year. And they all play! All the time. I have thirteen kids, and they all bat in order. And they all play, all the time. Six in the infield and everybody else in the outfield; seven outfielders, none of whom want to be out there. It's the law in Ridgewood baseball at this level. Hmmm. Maybe with seven I could just, like, lay them end to end out in the outfield and form some sort of impenetrable shield to stop the forward progress of ground balls.

Hey! Someone did hit the ball. B.A.

"Watch it, Monique!" God, she's going to get killed out here. I make a mental note to have a talk with Monique's mother. Maybe she'd be happier like, you know, Not Playing! Maybe she's just playing because of peer pressure. You shouldn't *force* a child to play. Could be a traumatic, and in her case, a boneshattering experience.

The ground is sopping wet. The baseball gets muddy. My ninety-dollar Nikes! Ruined.

"Can we go now?" asks Monique, dressed to play baseball in some sort of MTV Slut Wear for Juniors.

Andy slams a ball. Hey! Willie fields it cleanly—all right!—and throws to first . . . to . . . Jean . . . who leaps out of the way before the ball gets to her. Just in time. She might have been hurt.

"Mr. Geist," she says, "I don't want to play first base. I'm lousy."

Her mother is still standing on the sidelines, poised to call her lawyer on the car phone. "Look," I tell her mother. "This is inhumane. Lethal injection would be better."

My co-coach, Gerald Meeks, shows up at 5:25, five minutes before practice is over, greets me and pulls a couple of the kids aside. Starts telling Anand and Lynne about the infield fly rule. Oh-oh. He's been reading *Coaching Youth Baseball.*

Those books have, like, *whole chapters* on sliding into second base. Incredibly technical, nerdy stuff. Which may be why it appeals to Gerald.

A lot of coaches wind up trying to tell the kids everything in the book! Consequently, the important things are forgotten (or completely disregarded) by the kids right along with the unimportant when the ball is put in play. "See, kids, the *principle* behind the infield fly rule is. . ."

I walk away for a while. When I return, he's saying: "So, you see, Monique, a balk can be performed in fifty different ways, number forty-seven being. . ."

We tell them what they don't need to know, and we tell them too much, period:

"Eye on the ball, bat back, watch it spin, feet wide apart as the shoulders, shoulders level, hands together, knuckles lined up, keep your rear foot farther from plate than the front foot, that's good but keep your weight forward on the balls of your feet but a bit more on the rear foot, chin tucked, hands up, and even with and slightly behind the rear shoulder about six inches out . . ."

Yikes! "You know, Gerald," I say, "we really need to be telling most of these kids to keep their gloves on and which general direction to run in after they hit the ball. Not quite so much, today anyway, on the infield fly rule."

I keep it simple. On fielding I tell them to get ready, get in front of the ball, keep their gloves down and keep their butts down. (They love the part about keeping their butts down.) Step and throw.

In batting, I reduce it pretty much—except in special cases—to: eye on the ball, hands together on the bat, watch the ball hit the bat, run like hell and don't stop 'til you're past the bag!

For the advanced, like Byron: swing early and

try to hit the ball to left field, because most nine—and ten-year-old third basemen can't throw you out with any regularity and because it will help you swing soon enough. They all swing a little late, and if you hit the ball to the first baseman, who doesn't even have to throw the ball, you're usually out.

I always play my best fielder at first base. Willie. Most kids at that age swing late and hit it that way. Also, most of the throws are less than perfect, to say the least, and you need a guy to stop the ball, because if it gets past him, the runner gets an extra base. The rule of thumb on the glove? Big enough to boat a flopping sea bass.

Certain things, they can't get into their heads that first year or so, like when they have to tag a runner, and when the runner is forced out. Or when a fly ball is caught they have to come back and tag up before they run to the next base. Forget it!

Tax assessor or no tax assessor, Neville will be killed in the infield. Hermie is worse. "Look out, Hermie! I don't want you getting hurt out there."

"No problem," said B.A. "His old man's an ambulance chaser."

"Hermie. Your dad's a . . . personal injury lawyer?

"Yeah."

"Outfield! Deep center."

One day! Two hours of practice! Our only hope is that the opposition is worse.

All B.A. is doing is slowly rounding the bases. "I'm trying to figure out my home run trot for this year. I like to do it so it really pisses off the other team, you know?"

Charlie is teaching the other kids the trick play, the oldest play in the book. You know, the one where a runner is at first and the pitcher acts like he has the ball but really the first baseman still has it and when the runner moves off the bag, the first baseman tags him out? A classic, and it still works sometimes.

Danny can field but instead of throwing the ball to the first baseman, he prefers to run over and drop it on first base.

Willie is practicing his spitting.

Lynne hits the ball and runs to third base. Oh boy!

"Looks like it might be a long season," I say to Gerald.

"Well," he replies, "my team didn't win a game last year, but the youngsters had some fun and learned some basic decent human values."

Swell.

THE OPENING DAY PARADE

There is a Friday night in April that is almost like Christmas Eve for kids in our town.

It is the night before the Little League parade, which kicks off the baseball season in our town. My kids never sleep all that well on that Friday night—visions of baseballs dancing in their heads.

A coach in a nearby town takes a long three-hour drive in his car the night before opening day to calm his nerves.

Some children sleep in their uniforms—truly! Hats and all! Others have been wearing their uniforms to school all week. Most are satisfied to just lay out everything neatly on a chair—cap, team T-shirt, jeans, white socks and new, shiny black baseball shoes—so they can jump into them and get to that parade on time.

They wake early—a few in the predawn hours—don their uniforms and try to rouse their parents. And who's kidding whom? Some of the parents are up too—some almost as excited as the kids.

The kids begin arriving an hour early, gathering in the parking lot of the commuter train station. Those ten and up might arrive on their bikes, but these are suburban kids and most of them are dropped off—sometimes by mothers in nightgowns.

It is vintage Norman Rockwell and a colorful kaleidoscope as the parking lot fills with kids commingling in their shirts of red, yellow, orange, green, blue, maroon. The uniforms are usually half small and half extra large. They fit no one in the league and all the kids want the same couple of numbers, although they can't explain why.

Our team color this season is baby blue. If you have anything to say about it, avoid baby blue as your team color. In our town they call it "Columbia blue," after Columbia University. But they might as well call it "baby blue"; most kids associate Columbia athletics with its football team, which recently set a national record for consecutive losses. In any event, it's tough to win—psychologically—with baby blue caps and shirts. I have seen pink! Dark blue is good, so is red. Green and maroon are fine. Yellow, not so hot.

Also, the name of your team is important. Living with baby blue is one thing, playing games with the words "Ridgewood Corset Shop" emblazoned across the front and back is quite another—yet one team has to live with it every year.

I liked it the year we were Ridgewood Hardware. Our color was dark blue, too. Solid name, solid color. We won the League championship and took the plaque to the hardware store. The owner was appreciative, but offered nary a single free phillips-head screwdriver or anything.

I wasn't crazy about it the year we were the Van der Steere and Young Fighting Realtors, but. . . we didn't do badly. Some sponsors will reward the team for victories. Renato's Pizza, for example, donated a couple of pies to our postseason party, if memory serves me right.

Our team sponsor this year is the Curl Up 'N' Dye hair salon. It used to be Leo's Barber Shop, run by Leo and Ruth, until Ruth suggested they do nails and Leo ran off with the manicurist. Ruth changed the name. Leo always gave 50 percent off on haircuts to all members of the team he sponsored, and mothers used to *beg* their kids to not take advantage of the offer. Leo had no scissors, just the electric shears. Learned his trade in the service. You walked out of Leo's, you could go directly to basic training at Fort Dix. But nowhere else. Not for a week or so. That team always looked like they'd just been in for group brain surgery.

You look around at the parade. God, are Luke and David and John all on the same team? How did that happen? They cheat.

"We're gonna kill your team," Luke yells, as he passes by. Nice guy. He was on my team last year. We went through a lot on that team; I guess bygones are bygones.

As parents and coaches schmooze, the kids grow progressively more restless and begin stealing caps and spitting water. The thirteen- and fourteen-year-olds, who have marched in the parade for four, five and six years, wear Walkmen and don't want to be here. They sneak off as soon as they can after attendance is taken. It's embarrassing for them, marching with these little kids. I mean, think of it. Willie's little sister four years younger is in the *same parade*! A lot of them march about one block, pop into Bagelicious and hang out.

The coaches have put the names of their teams on poster boards for the parade: Tarvin Realtors, Burger King, Dr. Godart's Plaque Attackers, Woofery Dog Grooming, C. C. Van Emburgh Funeral Parlor, Bagelicious.

And there are the dignitaries. Bowie Kuhn, the former Commissioner of Major League Baseball, used to be up there at the head of the parade. He lived in Ridgewood until he fled for Florida to elude creditors, or so the rumors go.

And of course, there were other dignitaries: The Commissioner of the Ridgewood Baseball Association, Barney Foozle, maybe a school board member, occasionally the mayor himself.

Finally came the single wail of a siren, and the police car moved out with lights flashing, dignitaries close behind, followed by hundreds and hundreds of ballplayers. There is a battle on each team over which two kids get to hold the sign. No more than about one hundred people watch the parade and they are spread out over a mile-long parade route. Of the hundred people, a good 50 percent have camcorders.

By the halfway point, the kids start asking if it's their turn to hold the sign. Others need to go to the bathroom. Still others want to go into stores and buy candy; one even asks as we pass the theater if he can go in and catch a movie or at least buy one of those seven-pound packs of Twizzlers.

Most of the spectators are bunched up at the end of the parade near the bandshell, where the children gather and watch the opening ceremonies.

Someone throws out the first ball. Each and every dignitary gives a little speech on the importance of fair play and learning values and the need to have fun.

"We would if you'd shut up!" someone yells. Oh God, it was one of mine.

GAME ONE

The first games traditionally begin right after the parade. Ready or not. Oh boy. Who is to play in what positions? And a batting order? It seemed hopeless.

Well, let's see. B.A.'s our cleanup hitter, definitely. If Andy ever gets his weight behind one, which seems unlikely, it could go a long way. Bat him fifth. Willie's a good hitter, he'll hit first. Second? Danny, maybe? Third could be Charlie. That's fine. But what happens after that? Neville, Hermie, Jean, Lynne, Emily, Monique and . . . Anand. Aieee! Like a thousand miles of bad road.

B.A. on the mound, but rules stipulate he can only pitch three innings. Six-inning games, Charlie pitching after him? Maybe put Andy behind the plate, he can't catch the ball, but a natural backstop. Willie and the big glove at first. Hermie at second; I mean, he can't throw any farther than second to first. Charlie at third—he's the only one except B.A. who can even throw it from third to first. Accuracy? Zero. But you can't have everything. Shortstop? Neville? Tax assessor! Neville it is. The rest of 'em we'll scatter willy-nilly in the outfield; hope the ball just hits one of them and stops.

Of course I'd been thinking about our first game all week. I had been carrying around an extra legal pad, tucked under the one I'm always carrying for business matters, and sort of secretively writing down potential batting orders and various fielding alignments. $E = MC^2$ must have been a snap compared to figuring out how to play each kid the requisite two innings in the infield without giving the game away.

Anand in the infield? Sounds like the working title for a disaster film. Can't pitch, obviously, due to his inability to throw. First base was out of the question. Can't catch. Second? Can't field. Likewise, couldn't put him at short. Now, third base seemed like a possibility. Since even the best of players infrequently fields a ball at third and throws it to first in time to get the runner out, why not just concede a ball hit to third as a hit?

Catchers never make put-outs at home either, so Monique could catch. Wrap her in all that equipment and stick her behind the plate. Sure. Who cares if it takes two minutes for her to retrieve each pitch and throw it back to—somewhere in the vicinity of?—the pitcher.

Our first game was with Ridgewood Corset Shop immediately after the parade. Tough team, coached by Lefty. His son, Righty, was a good little athlete. We coached a lot of games against each other in a variety of sports, always close, games which Lefty thought had some sort of sociological significance because he lived in the prefab part of town.

I liked Lefty. He coached his kids well, took them to the batting cages and played dirty when he had to.

Judging from warmups, he didn't seem to have too strong a contingent this year. But, then, just how good did they have to *be*?

The top of the order in any batting lineup is always tough, then it always seems to tail off to three or four people at the bottom of the order who almost always strike out. This season I was worried we were going to have eight people like that at the "bottom" of our order—everybody after B.A. McCarthy.

He walked the first batter on four pitches to open the season. He was nervous.

"Calm down, Byron!" I shouted. He glared at me. "Calm down, B.A." I corrected. "Just throw it to . . . uh . . . Hey Gerald, who'd you put inside that heap of catcher's equipment I see behind the plate? Monique? B.A., just throw it to Monique like you were playing catch. Forget that the batter is even there."

And B.A. did begin pitching balls in the general vicinity of home plate. The batters responded by swinging wildly at pitches a foot over their heads or rolling across the plate. He struck out the second batter and the third batter before Righty hit a ball very hard into the outfield, which proved tantamount to introducing a cat at a dog show.

Hermie jumped out of the way just in time or the ball would have hit him. Lynne stood up from the kneeling position and gave chase to the ball, as did Andy. But, alas, Jean picked it up and threw a sort of misfire that took off from her hand and traveled on a forty-five-degree angle for about ten feet. Whereupon Anand and Danny both tried to pick it up; Anand first reaching for it, then realizing that Danny had reached for it first, and both politely stepping back to allow the other to pick up the ball, as Righty crossed home plate.

Two-nothing. This wasn't going to be pretty.

Rattled, B.A. walked the next batter and Lefty began yelling "Make it be your pitch," which was a thinly disguised code for: "Stand there and hope to walk. It's the only chance you little bums have got." The next two batters also walked.

Time out. I walked to the mound slowly and deliberately the way I'd seen big league managers do. I may have spit a couple of times.

"B.A.," I said, "these guys aren't *ever* going to swing, so just throw it over the plate." He did, striking out the next batter for the third out.

"Can't just stand there with the bat on your shoulder!" Lefty shouted at the batter who'd struck out—the one he'd instructed not to swing.

I had a warm spot in my heart for Lefty, but I was starting to hate him—just a little.

Now it was our turn at the plate. An anxious moment. If the top of our lineup couldn't hit, we were finished for the season.

"Willie, Danny, Charlie, B.A.!" I shouted. "Those are our first four batters."

Actually we never got to the first four batters, because the first three struck out. Ugh!

B.A. held the Corsetteers scoreless in the second inning, then led off in the bottom of the inning, smashing the first ball pitched to him over the left-field fence—home run! All the kids lined up to greet him at home plate. Two-to-one. Little Leaguers love a homer. They pounced on B.A., and jumped up and down.

Monique nearly—*very* nearly—kissed him on the mouth. Didn't see *that* addressed on the Little League video.

B.A was up for it, no doubt. He was a stud. He was Out There, you know what I mean? He had earned the admiration of everybody in the elementary school by going to J. J. Winberie's family restaurant and telling the waitress it was his birthday, getting a complimentary dinner, complimentary cake and a serenade by the waiter-waitress mixed chorus. His birthday was still six months away.

My daughter liked him but wouldn't admit it. The most handsome, refined boy in the school liked her, but she didn't like him. Oh no! *She* liked Bad Ass McCarthy.

Unfortunately, the next three batters—Andy, Hermie and Neville—went down on strikes.

Again, Byron held the Corsetteers scoreless in the third, but, in the bottom half of the inning, Lynne and Jean struck out, Emily walked (Hey!) and Monique—guess what?—struck out. She is one of those who has to be *informed* that she is out. "Uh, young lady, that's three strikes," the umpire says as she stands there with a glazed look on her face. I have to go up to the plate: "Nice try, honey, but that's three strikes, so that's it for right now."

Uh-oh. Fourth inning. Have to change pitchers. It's the law. Little League Elbow.

Also I had to move some of the weaker kids into the infield to give them their mandatory two innings. Willie refused to pitch, as did several of the other boys.

We gave Andy the ball. He got off to a rough start. His first pitch was three feet too high. The second bounced and rolled across the plate. The third was of a proper height, but to the wrong side of the batter. He walked his first three batters. In our league, you cannot walk in any runs, so once the bases are loaded the pitcher has carte blanche to just throw the ball as hard as he wants until finally the batter hits the ball or strikes out. In most cases, with the pitcher throwing his hardest, the batter strikes out.

Or is hit by the ball. Andy hit three kids. The first two kids cried. With the third kid hit, both the batter and Andy cried.

Four-to-one.

Charlie took the mound and quickly showed that he could throw the ball over the plate, but . . . very . . . very . . . sl-oooow-ly. Righty hit a grand slam, Lefty looked smug. Hate the guy. We had Byron and Willie doing their required time in the outfield at the time so when Righty hit the ball deep we still had a chance. Willie fired it into the infield, which normally would have held Righty to a double, except. . . *Monique* was on the receiving end! The ball very narrowly missed decapitating her, then rolled in under the catcher, portrayed by Anand, who could not see with a mask on, could not move in all that equipment and was still turning around like a dog trying to lie down and fumbling around with his hand underneath himself trying to locate the ball as Righty crossed the plate.

Charlie's slooooow-pitch style, coupled with our current defensive (if you will) alignment was a lethal combination, and by the time we were out of the inning the score was 27–1.

"OK," I said, "nobody hangs his head here. Twenty-six runs and we're right back in this thing!"

Anand struck out. Willie singled. Yes! (Ultimately what you really care about is how well your own kid is doing.) Danny struck out, the little bastard. I. . . didn't mean that. Charlie actually hit the ball well, a fly ball into short center, but you know what? The little son-of-a-bitch on the other team caught it!

"Who wants to pitch?" I said, loudly enough for all to hear. When you are losing, or winning, a game by twenty-six runs you can play the part of the Good Sport. And you want everybody to realize that you *are* a good sport. Maybe that's why he's losing by twenty-six runs. He's a good sport, letting all the kids play and everything. What a guy that ol' Bill Geist is! A real prince, I'll tell ya.

"Willie?" He shook his head.

"Oh, please, please, please, please, pleeeease!" begged Jean, who you could tell was unaccustomed to not getting her way.

She took the mound, promptly walked three batters in a row on an astounding array of pitches rarely if ever witnessed in the annals of baseball, including several behind the backs of the batters.

But mostly, they traveled about halfway to the batter and rolled to a stop somewhere near home plate. "Directionally, not too bad," Meeks commented.

With Anand behind the plate, dusk began to settle. Each pitch took quite a while to retrieve and to return in the general direction of the mound.

Jean threw about forty pitches to the next batter. She was incapable of throwing a ball that could be hit or could even conceivably be swung at or even one that might hit a batter. The outfield sat down first. "Stay in the ready position!" Coach Meeks demanded. "Keep working hard out there, kids! Keep working hard!"

I couldn't help smiling a little when the infielders began taking off their gloves, chatting with their parents on the sidelines, that type of thing. A keen Little League manager can detect these subtle signs and knows when to make his move.

I extracted Jean and brought in Emily. Now, it could have been the gathering darkness, or even instruction from Lefty to end this thing, but sweet little Emily struck out the side! "Are you from Taiwan or what?" I asked.

"Yes," she answered softly.

♦ ♦ ♦

Bottom of the fifth: "Hey that's the same kid out there pitching; been out there all game! Lefty, he can only pitch three innings—you know that!—and he's already pitched four!"

"Sorry, Bill, don't get excited," Lefty said. "An oversight on my part."

He brought in his back-up pitcher, who was warming up throwing the ball *underhand*!

"Oversight, my fat ass," said Andy, watching their underhanded relief pitcher. I nodded in agreement. *Not* what they'd tell you to do at the clinic.

B.A. hit the first underhanded pitch into left center field for a home run! A Little League home run, at any rate. Maybe a couple of errors in there someplace.

I quieted the kids down after they celebrated the home run and gave them my first inspirational talk: "The secret in Little League is this: Never Stop Running!"

Andy got all of his weight into one and the ball went . . . forever. It had to. Forever, as Johnny Mathis pointed out, is a long long time, but barely long enough for Andy to make it all the way around the bases.

And he'd already stated he couldn't slide, because he keeps his cache of Hershey's bars in his back pockets.

Tiny Herm hit the ball four feet in front of the plate, which, as it turns out, is one of the very best hits in Little League baseball, because the pitcher can't get to it in time and the catcher—imprisoned in all that equipment—would have to be Harry Houdini to get to it in time.

Bunting was outlawed at this level, but the umpire couldn't lay a glove on Herm for bunting because he was swinging as hard as he could and that's all the power Herm had, that's all. The power would come. No it wouldn't.

Neville walked. "Good eye!" Lynne walked. Jean walked. Can't walk in any runs, we need a hit. Emily . . . homered! Hit the ball cleanly between the outfielders and ran the bases so fast she had to push Jean and Lynne across the plate to get them out of her way. Wow. "All right Emily!"

B.A. gave this . . . girl! . . . a look. A stare of disbelief.

Monique, God bless her, walked. Anand struck out. "Wait for your pitch, Anand, know what I mean?" Willie "homered"—as it were—and we were on our way. Danny walked—"Good eye!"—Charlie tripled and B.A. hit his second home run of the inning! Would wonders never cease?

There is a rule—called the slaughter rule—in our league that no batter can bat more than once in an inning. But I had . . . forgotten! . . . to invoke the rule when the Corsetteers were slaughtering us, and Lefty had forgotten to bring it up. Another oversight. He knew he couldn't raise the issue now.

The sixth inning was not played. Lefty, suddenly a stickler for the rules, did invoke the rule stating that no inning can commence after the nearest automatic street light comes on.

We lost a heartbreaker, 27–26.

DISCREET PEST CONTROL

Game Two was Wednesday at 4:00 P.M.

Yes, one *must* pretty much give up one's job to coach Little League. Or try to get something on the midnight shift.

Once Daylight Saving Time rolls around the games begin at 6:00 P.M., which isn't a lot better. You have to be there by 5:30 to warm up and everything.

The only times I ever turned in one of my newspaper columns on time was during the Little League season when I had to be home for games. They were the only things in life important enough to make me do that.

And many was the time when I'd have to leave a game for half an inning, to drive seventy miles per hour through town to get to the pay phone at the 7-Eleven to make the obligatory call to the copy desk for questions on my column. The editors always knew something was up. Those were the only times I wouldn't fight to the death over every little change they'd made. "Oh, you removed the first three paragraphs?" I'd say. "Fine, fine. Well so long, and have a nice day."

And many was the day I was caught in traffic on the West Side Highway, or on a commuter bus in the Lincoln Tunnel, thinking about those thirteen kids in their little uniforms standing around home plate getting ready to forfeit because the coach was late.

Such was the case in our second game of the season. I was stuck in rush-hour traffic on the turnpike and so was my co-coach. My wife, Jody, showed up in the nick of time to stand in as coach and start the game. The opposing coach, Bud Flint, who played by the book (when it served his purposes—moral integrity in Little League being a strategy to be employed when and where it serves you), took issue with this, saying that my wife was not the Coach of Record—whatever the hell that meant—and he said he was playing the game under protest.

Hate that guy. But he argued the point long enough that I made it to the game wearing my suit and tie and a blood-pressure-red complexion from running for almost a mile from the bus stop to the game.

I was there in time to hear Flint tell his team: "The road to Williamsburg begins here!" Either this game had some sort of historic significance in American history I was unaware of, or he meant "Williams*port.*"

I had made some adjustments for Game Two with Flint's team, Discreet Pest Control. The first thing I did was to make Emily Chang our leadoff hitter. She could hit and she was fast, a veritable Rickey Henderson of the Orient, not to mention the female gender.

We were supposed to leave the batting order the same the entire way through the season, but almost *nobody* was that straight—except Yo Norb and my co-coach, who asked about it. "But, but . . . she doesn't bat first, she . . ." He didn't quite *get it.* I ignored him until he went away.

To shore up our defense, which did, after all, relinquish twenty-seven runs in five innings in the first game, I moved one outfielder to a position not far behind second base so that when a ball was hit there and there was a runner on first, the short center fielder could (ideally) field the ball and tag second base for a force out. That defensive move worked well and was adopted by every team in the league. The real cheaters, like your Knaverys, put the short center fielder *on* second base until the opposing coach protested, and if the other coach happened to be, say, Yo Norb, well the fielder just played the whole game there. The rule states the outfielders must be at least fifteen feet behind the basepath, but an oversight is an oversight.

B.A. and Emily would be our pitchers. I reiterated that they should fire the ball as hard as they wished and anywhere they wished once the bases were loaded; and to the more cautious members of the squad, I reiterated the rule of baserunning: Never Stop.

"Do you think we should begin with a team prayer?" Meeks asked.

"If we lose again today, definitely," I replied. "Might want to sacrifice a player or two, as well."

There were a few grievances, most of them concerning prolonged stays in the outfield.

"And I want to be moved in the batting order,"

Hermie complained. "I have to bat behind Andy and there's chocolate all over the bat."

"Dork!" Andy retorted.

"Try batting a few games with the chocolate on the bat, Herm," I advised. "Could work like pine tar."

Emily stepped to the plate in the top of the first. The pitcher turned and yelled to his fielders: "It's a girl!"

Coach Flint gave some sort of hand signal for the infield to move in, which they did—much to my amazement. "Well-disciplined children," Meeks said. He was impressed. Meeks was really getting on my nerves. He said it in a way that let me know he thought our team was *not* well-disciplined. He said "well-disciplined children" like you and I might say "well-marbled meat" or something. I don't know.

There were more murmurs of "Move up, it's a girl," and finally this little—how to describe him?—this little *prick* on the other team delivered the first pitch and Emily stroked the ball to deep left center and was crossing home plate by the time they picked it up!

"It's a girl all right!" I shouted at Flint. He was humiliated. His basic stand on girls is that, well, girls are OK to stand on and that's about it. He had stated publicly that girls ought to have their own leagues and should not "bastardize" boys' baseball. You know, mongrelize.

I thought before the next game about moving Emily to a power hitter's position, maybe third or fifth in the order—maybe even cleanup hitter. But I loved having her as the Great Demoralizer right at the outset.

Our whole team hit well in this game. I told them they all looked a little nervous at the outset of the first game and that they should relax when they were batting and not worry so much about failing.

Kids think they're supposed to hit the ball every time they get to the plate or they're failures—all part of the instant gratification thing we teach them so well.

"Don Mattingly just signed a contract for nineteen million bucks and he only gets a hit once every three times at the plate. Most all of you are doing as well as that!"

I also told Meeks to stop yelling batting tips to them as they were hitting. Best Little League coach I ever saw never talked during games and forbade yelling things at the batter while he was at the plate. Yogi Berra once said: "You can't hit and think at the same time." I am not hitting now and I think he was right.

Their team did not hit at all well. Flint could not possibly stop himself from coaching:

"Choke up!

"Bat back.

"Back elbow up.

"Bend those knees.

"Eye on the ball.

"Don't swing at high ones; watch the low ones, the umpire's calling those strikes today."

Flint's kids were always busy processing that last piece of data when the ball went by.

His team was extremely well-disciplined, period. He had an intricate system of signs, telling his runners when to steal. Meeks didn't like my system, in which I'd yell out loud from the dugout: "Steal second on the next pitch!" It worked for me.

Andy didn't pitch this time. Nor Jean. Emily came on and pitched three innings with no earned runs. There were a few unearned, but only eight.

We won Game Two, 15–8.

I got into a row with Flint's charming assistant coach, Sylvia. She is a not-altogether-unattractive blonde who likes to play by what she calls "the honor system." That is: when the umpire makes a call against her team, she wants *me* to change the call. Flint was so impressed with this quality last season that he asked her to be one of his assistant coaches.

For example, in this game their player hits a ball down the right field line. The umpire calls it foul. Sylvia comes out on the field and yells "Bill! C'mon. That was fair. You saw it!" I do not argue the call with the umpire. I tell her I try not to argue the calls with the umpires. "OK, if that's the way you want to win! Go ahead." She does this on three calls in a row. She tells all the kids on her team that our team is cheating. She tells the parents we are cheating. The kids will not shake our hands after the game. She calls The Commissioner!

One would think that a policy of not arguing with the umpires and letting them call the game would be a sound approach. Nope. That doesn't work either.

Coach Flint reiterated that he was protesting the game because my wife had officially started the game and not me. I hate that guy. The previous loss he'd protested because the catcher was not using an official catcher's mitt, but rather just a fielder's mitt. Last year he protested because kids on the other teams allegedly hadn't touched the bag, left a base too early, or threw their bats. He was a letter-of-the-law man, when it suited his purposes, a common trait among Little League coaches.

We didn't care. Curl Up 'N' Dye was playing .500 ball now, carrying a winning streak, a winning smudge anyway, into the next game. We were on a roll.

JIFFY LUBE

There would be no arguments at Game Three. The opposing team was Jiffy Lube, its coach one Big Bill Shoulders, a police officer in town, who wore T-shirts with a variety of sadistic messages on them.

For tonight's game he had selected: "Kill 'Em All—And Let God Sort' Em Out."

Also, he had a pistol strapped to his ankle! Yes!

Poor Shoulders. He desperately wanted to be a SWAT-team type, breaking down doors in *48 Hours,* making drug busts, yelling: "It's goin' down!"

Instead, here he was making the lives of housewives more difficult by stopping them for going five miles per hour over the speed limit taking their kids to ballet and skating classes.

Shoulders had built quite a reputation for giving speeders severe tongue lashings, and when they objected, he had no qualms about slapping them up against the car and cuffing them! Gotta do it.

He's a real Just Say No to Expired Parking Meters guy, too. Takes it very seriously. He'll give you a good tongue lashing for that: "You were supposed to be back here five minutes ago. But no!"

I had a beer with Shoulders after a game once, and only once, and he told me he doesn't really believe in the court system. By that I don't mean he's lost faith in it; rather, Shoulders doesn't believe we should *have* one.

Also, I could not argue with the umpire, with whom I'd had an altercation the year before. In that game, against Attractive Above Ground Pools, we'd been getting bad calls all game, when I found out the guy was the uncle of a kid on the other team, for chrissake! He was, like, *winking* at the other bench. When he called my son out on a called strike in the bottom of the final inning with our team trailing by a run, I'd had all I could take: "Stick around for their team picture, ump!"

He threw me out of the game, but it was already over—Thanks Be to Him.

But he still reported me to The Office of The Commissioner, who maddens coaches by speaking to them as if he were speaking to kindergartners. Make that preschoolers. "Now, Bill, we all get involved in these games, and of course human nature itself along with our social conditioning has us wanting to win, wanting to win, but we must all control ourselves so as to set a good example for the children of this country."

We humor Barney by listening. Except the time a frustrated parent on a losing team reported that Lefty had given one of his players a pat on the rear end after the player hit a home run—the Concerned Parent insinuating there was something *wrong* with that. Barney was actually going to hold a hearing on the matter, until several of us implored Barney not to do that. Plus, Shoulders threatened to kick Barney's butt if he did.

Oh. We won the game! But not without incident.

Smash Danner struck out Danny, who commenced to have a temper tantrum, beating the ground around the plate with a bat for several minutes, before dropping it—whew!—and rolling around on the ground.

I put my arm around Danny and tried to get him to quiet down. After the game, his (fat) mother chewed me out unmercifully for interfering with him while he was "working through" his problems. She reported me to The Commissioner's Office. She and The Commissioner were close friends, as it turned out. Foozle became confused and thought that what she was saying made sense, since her explanation contained popular phraseology such as "working through problems."

Danny was transferred to another team. Apparently his father had been lobbying with Foozle to get him off my team. This (idiotic) previous husband of the aforementioned (fat) mother called me at work one day from Seattle, where he was living with his (thinner, equally indiscriminate) new wife and told me: "How can you play your son at first base when my son is the best first baseman on the team, I'm telling you right now." His powers of perception were awesome—as my kids would say—given his perspective from three thousand miles away. (With my kids, everything in the world is either "awesome" or it "sucks.")

Lynne got her first hit of the season. She arrived

late, coming directly from ballet class. It's hard to say exactly how it happened, but she somehow connected with a high pitch and it sailed down the right field line for a home run. She circled the bases, still wearing her tutu, which was sticking out the top of her shorts. Nice touch. The poor opposing pitcher was mortified. He threw down his glove and stomped on it.

And poor Shoulders. He backed Flint in his stand against having girls in "the boys' league"—and Shoulders had the firepower to back it up!

Lynne's mother cheered wildly, while Shoulders burned. Next time her meter expired, she was history.

GIRLS (AND WHAT TO DO ABOUT THEM)

Hitting home runs in tutus! If you think Emily got a look from B.A. after her home run, you should have seen the one he gave Lynne!

I have coached teams of all boys, teams of boys and girls, and all-girl teams. I love the girls' teams. Girls are just so . . . so . . . *different,* you know? (You might want to mark that one with your yellow highlighter.)

OK. I *didn't* play catch with my daughter as much as I did with my son. Shoot me.

The truth of it is, Libby and I only go out and play catch in the yard a couple of times a year. The last time we played catch in the yard, she wanted to pitch. Overhand. Hardball.

I crouched and she tried to throw strikes, but mainly she wanted to spit. Like Willie, she likes the nuances of the game, especially the disgusting ones. She'd spit two or three times before each pitch. It's not easy spitting that much. "How do the guys on TV do it so much, Dad?" she asked. I told her about chewing tobacco and wads of bubble gum and all that stuff the pros use so they can spit really, really well. I told her that sometimes they put wads of chewing tobacco and snuff and bubble gum and sunflower seeds all together in one big wad. "Gross!" she replied.

We didn't play catch as much. She wasn't as well prepared to play Little League baseball as was my son, not by a long shot.

Second, she is our second child. And seeing that even with all the pressure we applied on our son, he was still probably not going to make it to the major leagues, we backed off a little on the second child, as parents so often do. With the second one, it's more like you want them to enjoy life than dominate it.

Plus, she threw just a little bit funny. Girls throw

a little funny. I know! Girls Don't Throw Funny. And yet. . .

But! She could field a ball with the best of the boys, so she played hardball when she was eight and nine years old, instead of playing in the girls' softball league.

There are problems peculiar to the girls' game, like fake fingernails and baseball gloves, bangs and baseball caps. Ponytails can present problems, not to mention barrettes.

In a key situation in a softball game, Lynne blasted a triple, but was tagged out as she strolled off the bag looking for a lost earring. Batting helmets play hell with earrings. After our practices, it's like contact lens time again, with everybody down on all fours on the basepaths, looking for earrings. Lynne's lost earring was a valuable pearl one, a family heirloom, worn (one presumes) to set off her "Let's Go Mets" T-shirt.

Boys come to the girls' games and stand on the sidelines watching—a sight Betty Friedan would love.

I mean, hell, you don't really want them out there just cheerleading for the boys, all short skirts and fake smiles, do you? The hell of it is, Libby probably wants to do that. But she won't. Not because she shares my values. She can't do a cartwheel. Neither can I. Never could.

The girls do love to win every bit as much as the boys, and parents are no less crazed at the girls' games. Every bit as awful. Same skulduggery at the draft, same list of names in the computers, a parent yelling F——you! at an opposing coach. Seeing all of this, you become more convinced than ever that it really *is* adults playing chess with the kids. Doesn't matter the gender of the chess pieces.

Some fathers want a son to play ball with so badly they have trouble adjusting to daughters. A neighbor of ours kept coming back from the hospital delivery room with what I thought was a bit of a hangdog expression: "Another girl," he'd sigh. Three times. Hey! Can't put 'em in little baskets and float 'em down the Yangtze River! I temporarily loaned him my son. We coached him together, until his girls started playing sports. All the sports; all the time.

Libby and Beth and Jessica and Maggie all played hardball the first year in the eight-year-old league, on our team: Tarvin's Fighting Realtors. That year, there was a girl on another team who brought her Barbie to a game.

Mostly, the four girls played the outfield, because there were six boys better than them who played the infield. Fathers pitch in the eight-year-old league, so, by pitching to the right spot at the right time, hits were achieved. And once the ball is struck in the eight-year-old league, it's pretty much a hit. Libby had a good first year. The next year there was a revolt at tryouts—Beth's father sparking a spontaneous stampede to sign up for softball—and most of the girls went.

Libby stuck with hardball. We had a good team so the other teams always had their best pitchers pitching against us. Libby got one or two hits the whole season. She was upset about this even after I pointed out that only about four boys ever hit the ball. One was a boy she liked. He hit the ball a lot. She was afraid he wouldn't like her if her batting average was too low. And she may have been right. But she was proud to be in the "boys' league" on a "boys' team."

She began not to swing at all, which was a good policy, actually, given that most of the pitchers fired the ball as hard as they could, but with a goodly degree of inaccuracy, often causing extensive "collateral damage" (as they say in the bombing trade) to spectators.

I didn't argue. I didn't want her growing up to be the East German hammer thrower type anyway, thank you.

Another girl, Jessica, always made Willie's all-star teams. She's still one of the cutest girls in town, but my son and his friends won't see her socially because she bumps them in the hallway and punches them in the arms and stuff. There was always the question: was she a token? She was an adequate fielder on the all-star team, but never hit much and along about the sixth grade or so, she drifted over into softball and became a star.

At ten, Libby opted for the girls' softball league.

She is a very good softball player—one of the very best in town of her age. My son's a very good baseball player, played on the all-star teams. In retrospect, I think she *enjoys* playing more than he does. With him, I was always there watching closely, being overly exuberant, perhaps, when he got a hit or made a play in the field; and a little disappointed when he didn't. Pressure. With her, she succeeds, she fails, she laughs and cries. It's not the end of the world in our society if girls aren't great in sports. They know it. But for a few years in the lives of boys, they really do believe they're second rate if they can't hit a ball, in much the same way that girls can be made to feel this way if they're not the object of the boys' attention. If you get a hit, your coach likes you, your teammates like you, your . . . father . . . likes you.

If you strike out you think they don't. And, the hell of it is, in too many cases, they really don't.

[illegible]

[illegible]

[illegible]

RAIN

sb

Game Four at beautiful Schwarzkopf Field. Rained out.

We were to have played Yo Norb's team, 0–2 on the season so far and falling fast.

Why is it always thus? That in baseball as in life, it's the easy games that get rained out. Remember this fundamental rule of Little League baseball: reschedule rainouts with crummy teams, not with the good ones.

If you can, and you probably can't. Last year, my daughter's softball team was so good, The Commissioner made us make up rainouts with good teams in place of our *scheduled* games with the bad teams. Never allowed us to play our two games with the worst team. Seemed a little fishy, like something cooked up between The Commissioner and Knavery.

Our game was scheduled for 3:00 P.M. Saturday. About 7:00 A.M., the kids begin calling: "Mr. Geist, are we going to play our game?"

"Not yet, it's still dark outside, isn't it? What time is it?"

"I don't know. But it's raining."

"We'll have to wait and see. I'll call you. OK?"

The phone rang all day. Most of the kids said things like: "Do we *have* to play baseball today? I'd rather play Super Mario Brothers." Some kids called four or five times. Hermie, as always, was particularly concerned. It rained until about noon, then stopped. Some mothers called and said they thought pneumonia was certain if the game went on. "I don't want Jeanie catching pneumonia in the rain." I know, I know. Or else you'll file a $1.7 million damage suit against me, Willard Scott and . . . God!

I called Yo Norb. "I really think we should play this game, Norbert." Then, realizing I sounded too eager, added: "The kids(!), Norb, the children, the youngsters really want to play this game."

Norbert thought it looked pretty bad out there. "And we can't take any chances," he cautioned.

"A child might be Struck-By-Lightning. We simply can't take that chance."

"I. . . I haven't seen any lightning, Norbert."

I told Yo Norb I'd go over at two o'clock and check the field. There was a little puddle in the batter's box, but that could easily be filled in with a shovelful of dirt. Little League coaches do a lot of groundskeeping during the early part of the season. One guy I know keeps several forty-pound bags of white powdery stuff, called True Flow or something, in his garage—stuff that's manufactured strictly for soaking up water on ballfields. Who says America doesn't make things any longer?

I called Norbert back to tell him it was not raining and that the field was fine. His wife, Virjean, answered.

"We have decided" (We? Norb, have you lost your *spine,* man?) "not to play. Besides the lightning, the grass may still be damp, and we cannot risk having a child fall and sustain serious injury."

Virjean drove me nuts! Just the way she said "child"; the way she said "sustain serious injury." Couldn't she just say "get hurt" instead of slipping on the grass and "sustaining serious injury"? Virjean was president of the PTA, and had led the successful drive to make all kids wear those stupid helmets when they ride their bikes to school. The result? Kids stopped riding their bikes, explaining they didn't want to "look like dorks." Accidents were averted.

Yes, Virjean, let's teach our children that *everything* in life is dangerous! No fun at all. More kids are injured falling down the steps than riding bikes, Virjean! Want to make kids put on helmets before they walk down the steps?!

Moreover, she wanted to eliminate pitching in Little League and make it all tee-ball. She didn't know we tried tee-ball and that kids like B.A. hit the ball so hard off a tee that infielders were sustaining injuries—*Serious* Injuries, Virjean. Serious! Playing the infield with B.A. hitting off a tee was like having a howitzer fired at you.

There was no arguing with her. "All right," I said, "but I would like to reschedule the game for next week." Perhaps some day when the humidity is not too high. Bitch.

So, I had twelve players to notify. They were disappointed. B.A.'s father had already dropped his son off at the field and he went on a tirade: "Jesus Christ! Can't play baseball when it's a little damp? Man, this whole town is a bunch of wussies, I'll tellya. Hell, back in Brooklyn, we shoveled snow off. . ."

Yeah, yeah, yeah. Just pick up your damned kid, will ya. You gotta cut these guys off or they'll start in about their days playing stickball, and the whole weekend's shot.

He raves on. "Christ, they cancel school in this town when there's heavy dew!"

Monique's mother was also beside herself. "Listen, I have *plans* for this afternoon. I made them weeks ago. I'm going to an important fashion show," she said moronically and oxymoronically, "and children are not invited. What am I supposed to do with Monique? I can't leave her home alone. *You* must not have any plans. You were going to be playing baseball from three to five anyway. I'll drop her off."

And when Monique's mother drops her off, I'm telling you, it's like a bombardier over Iraq. I swear she can drop off Monique without stopping the car, ejecting her at about thirty-five miles an hour so she doesn't have to alter her estimated time of arrival at the mall.

I couldn't reach most of the kids in time, and found them dropped off and huddled inside the bandshell.

◆ ◆ ◆

As we watched the rain come down and waited for parents to arrive, Hermie asked: "Did you play baseball, before you were old?" Thanks, Herm.

I told them my first baseball memory: receiving a full flannel uniform on my fifth birthday, and canvassing door to door for neighbors to admire it.

We played baseball in the neighbors' *biiig* backyard behind our house, I told them, a yard that has shrunk terribly in the wash of time. It was only about a tenth the size I remembered it when I drove by with my kids recently. Is it possible they moved all the houses closer together?

Neither my father nor my older brother played ball with me much. This is not cause for a weepy "About Men" column or anything, they just had better things to do. My brother was seven years older and wasn't about to stoop to the level of a squirt like me. My father played piano, not baseball.

All I wanted for my eighth birthday was to drop piano lessons, and my parents—already sensing that they probably did *not* have another Horowitz on their hands—mercifully pulled the plug on my musical career. They didn't want to prolong my suffering. Or theirs. "Oh," said B.A., "you sucked at piano?" Why yes, B.A. I did. . . suck.

From then on, it was "Play Ball!" We moved to a house with a big backyard of its own, and in a neighborhood of about two dozen kids—all just about my age, baby boomers all. The Foley Street gang.

For years to come, April through September, we played baseball in our backyard most every evening. My mother tried to plant trees in the yard, even putting up little chicken wire fences to protect them, but they were soon trampled—not surprisingly, since the trees themselves were often designated as bases.

Likewise, my parents' garden, in foul territory on the first base line, was pretty much "at risk," the tomatoes trampled into paste during the course of the season. My father's hopes for a nice lawn like the one on the Scott's grass seed box were likewise trampled underfoot.

You had to know the field. You could get extra-base hits by punching the ball over the corner of our ranch home, which jutted out into left field. Or you could line the ball under the Evanses' Buick next door. Or hit it to right field where the fielders would slip and slide on mulberries while you rounded the bases.

When New Yorkers do reminisce about their great stickball games, played without adult interference, with a car as first base and home runs that traveled a distance of three manhole covers—I understand completely.

Big Dan Armstrong, two years older and about a foot taller (six feet two inches), was the Babe Ruth of the Backyard. He could hit a ball to straightaway center field, out of our yard (short center), flying over the Evanses' yard (center and deep center), all the way into the Nelsons' yard. And on one historic evening, Big Dan hit one that rolled all the way to the Saxbys' yard. I swear to God. You could see the scorch marks on the ball from when it reentered the earth's atmosphere, and that's no lie.

Dan's sister, Kande, was a solid hitter and one of the cutest girls in town. She had it all.

"Did you like her?" asked Monique, and all the other kids went "Wuuuuuuu!"

"Did she have . . . " and B.A. cupped his hands over his chest.

Never mind! I snapped.

"Did she?" Lynne asked.

Eventually, yes.

Mom would open the back door—at her peril; it was right behind third base—and shout: "Dinner!" I'd tear into the back door just twenty feet from home plate—sweaty, dirty and out of breath—plop myself down and try to eat as fast as I could. My father would look down upon me as the swine that I was. My mother would suggest chewing. Then back out the door I'd go, still chewing.

"What did you do when it rained like this?" Emily asked.

We played Garage Ball, a fantastic game of my own invention that should have taken off in the marketplace and made me a millionaire, but (so far) has not. You go in the garage with a friend, a bat and a tennis ball and close the door. He pitches and you hit the ball as hard as you can and try to run to a base and back home before he can retrieve the careening ball and hit you with it.

Loved that game. Parents discouraged it. Said we broke things, which I argued was a moot point since everything breakable was already broken, including the pitcher's nose.

I kept statistics for our backyard baseball league: a running total of singles, doubles, triples and homers. A lot of the kids never knew I was keeping records, and one knew I was cooking the books.

Because she was beautiful, I allowed Kande to stay with me after the games and hit the ball for extra credit. (This also meant that she and I were the only ones out there together as darkness fell.) Kande would hit the ball and if I judged that it would have been a hit in the game, I gave her credit in the book. (If she kissed me under the weeping willow, I'd make it an extra base hit.)

"Wuuu!" went the kids.

I know, I know.

She finally dumped me anyway for one of Dan's friends who drove a cherry-red 1957 Chevy convertible. She was crazy to do that. Her stats dropped off the table, but somehow she didn't seem to care. The other kids were starting to drop out too; the neighborhood game was coming to an end.

Where the hell were the parents? I had called most of them and anyway there was, like, a monsoon going on here, and they don't realize the game has been called off?

I asked the kids if they ever played imaginary

baseball games, with themselves as the heroes, and most of the boys said they did. I've played a thousand of those games, like the ones Willie used to play in the backyard, and I must say: I have an outstanding won-lost record. I played a lot of baseball solitare when we stayed with my grandparents all summer. Sometimes I had a real ball, sometimes not. If the real ball was a tennis ball, so much the better. I could hit a tennis ball clear over their house—out of the park(!) as it were. Not to mention a golf ball. "That one is long gone, folks . . . a tremendous drive the likes of which we've never seen . . ."

I'd provide the play-by-play while trotting the bases, imitating Harry Caray, who was doing the Cardinal games in those days, a few miles away in Busch Stadium. I was humble, unsmiling, stalwart as I ran the bases after a homer, in the manner of Stan the Man.

"Who's that?" Andy asked, gnawing on a Hershey's.

"Musial, retard," Hermie replied.

Anyway, I just tried to be myself, Billy Geist, a superstar (although that term had yet to be coined), one of the best players in the majors—and one of the true gentlemen of the game! The games usually ended with a broken tomato vine and my ever-vigilant grandmother, Myrtle, stepping out the back door yelling: "Billy!" It was frightening.

Were she alive today, she would have seen Iraqis traipsing into Kuwait, opened the back door, thundered "Sadam!" and the entire Persian Gulf War would have been averted.

"But were you any good in Little League?" Hermie asked impatiently.

"The best," I replied, as honestly as I could.

Real baseball began with tryouts for Little League, when I was eight years old. Almost no one—other than coaches' sons and the locally legendary Chuck Hutchcraft—made the majors when they were eight, instead spending that first year in the Farm League on the Bears, Lions, Panthers or Rams, wearing a crummy cap and T-shirt.

Tryouts were nerve-wracking, and once they were over all you could do was go home and wait for . . . The Call.

I still wait for it. I never want to make The Call myself. I want people to Call Me. In high school and college, I waited for girls to call me. (I didn't date a lot.) In my career, I wait for the bosses to come to their senses (for chrissake!) and recognize genius! I wait a lot.

It took a couple of years—a *very* long time when you're eight, nine, ten years old—for that Little League call to come.

I'd go to the tryouts, and the coaches always seemed to say nice enough things—"nice catch," "nice throw," or (Arrgh!) "nice try." But even at that age you wonder: are they saying these things to everybody? Do their kind remarks correspond to those they're jotting down on those evaluation sheets? And is the guy saying these things just a helper, or does he have real clout?

"How'd it go?" my mom would ask when I returned from tryouts. She always asked so casually, either failing to recognize that this was the most important event of my life or perhaps knowing it was and trying to play it down.

"Really!" said Andy. He could relate.

"Good," I'd tell my mother. "I think." Then I'd go to my room, get on my knees, and pray: "Dear God, I know you're *probably* not supposed to pray for things like this, and I know you've probably overheard me saying that I don't like to go to church, but . . . Please! Please! Please! let me make a team

. . . and if I do, I'll never miss church again, EVER! I swear, and I will never ask for anything else for the rest of my life. Amen. P.S.: Bless the poor and the sick—right after you take care of this!"

A day later the phone rang. It was my friend George Hughes asking: "Do you know what team you're on?"

"Not yet," I said.

"They called me," he said. "I'm on Eisner's [Food Store]."

"Great!" I said.

Bill Murphy called. He was on Eisner's too. "Wouldn't it be great," he said, "if we all got on the same team?"

It sure would. My older brother Dave used to be on that team, back when it was the Piggly Wiggly (food store) Pirates. Red caps and red baseball socks. Good color.

Another day went by. I began to fret: "Any calls for me, Mom, while I was on the porch?" All the boys were talking about what teams they were on.

Then, finally, during dinner: "Billy. Phone's for you."

It was a man. All right! He said I was on his team. He sounded upbeat. He said he had heard I was good and he was glad to have me on his team!

"What team?" I asked, hoping it was Eisner's.

"Lions," he said.

My heart sank. A farm team. The minor league.

"Our first practice is Thursday," he said, filling the void. "See you then."

I hadn't made it. I didn't go back to the dinner table. I rushed to my room, closed the door, jumped face down on the bed and sobbed into the pillow.

We had all been equals in backyard games—George, Bill and me. Not anymore. Not in the opinion of Little League authorities, nor (apparently) in the eyes of . . . God.

So began a long, long run of not getting The Call. I embodied the Last Man Cut. When seventy-five kids tried out for the twelve-man ninth-grade basketball team, I was thirteenth.

In football, I was always cut on the last day. All my friends made the team. They'd sit around and tell the girls that they couldn't drink Cokes anymore because the carbonation was bad for their endurance. "Oh, reeeeeally?" the girls would coo.

You wait for The Call in life too. I waited for The Call for years in the suburban bureau of the *Chi-*

cago Tribune, the call to come downtown and work in the real office. The Call never came. When, after eight years (I mean, you don't even get *eight years* for manslaughter), the *New York Times* finally called instead, a colleague shouted: "There is a God!"

"So," B.A. asked, "did you quit? I wouldn't play on any dorky farm team."

I went to the minors and pitched for the Lions. As if the crummy little T-shirts and caps weren't bad enough, our color was yellow. I struck out everybody; I hit long home runs that rolled clear out into the bushes; I cried after the games.

At last, toward the end of that third season in the minors, the coach of U of I (University of Illinois) Drugs (Store)—I grew up in Champaign, Illinois—squad called to say his center fielder was going on vacation for the rest of the season (Hallelujah! Bon Voyage! Go With God!), and that he wanted me to take his place in the majors.

Nothing has ever felt better (well, there was the R and R in Bangkok) than putting on that real flannel uniform, shirt and pants. They were a little large, actually. That center fielder was a big guy.

And there were the real baseball stockings. Black. And cleats. Kids wore rubber cleats in the majors. There was a scoreboard and an outfield fence, and real dugouts. I didn't play an awful lot that year, but I was in The Bigs.

"You were lucky! Black is one bad ass color," B.A. said. He knows these things.

Walking home after a game, I'd always get some dirt out of a flowerbed someplace and wipe it on my pants and arms so I'd look like a valiant warrior returning from battle. Also, I didn't want my mother knowing I hadn't played and thinking "poor darling." I hated that.

"Really!" Andy interjected, unwrapping another Hershey's bar.

"Did you win the championship?" Hermie asked.

Well, when I was eleven, our team was pretty good. We had a big slugger who hit lots of homers.

"Like Mean Gene," said Willie.

(I'd forgotten Willie was there. Maybe I should embellish my own accomplishments a bit. I'd say that I batted .620 for the season when really it was just during the first half of the season. I finished at .475, actually, which meant I had quite a dip the second half.)

The next year, my last in Little League, we got a new coach who had a pair of eight-year-old twins.

They were shrimps. We were doomed. The coach played the twins in center and right field, which meant that for the most part any ball hit to the outfield was a homer. We went 1–17 that year, winning our only game of the year in semidarkness either in the bottom of the sixth or in extra innings, by one run, against the second-worst team in the league.

Eisner's Food Store was the team closest in ability to us, but that is like saying Mars is the closest planet. You still can't go there for lunch.

I was on the mound. Two outs. The coach told me to pitch the ball low so the big guy at bat, Jim Kerns, wouldn't hit a homer and win the game. I did, but he hit the ball high and deep anyway.

The kids in the bandshell held their breaths.

The left-fielder ran in front of one of the twins and caught the ball. We won!

U of I Drugs had a soda fountain, and the store offered us anything we wanted if and when we won a game. I think the owner was stunned when we showed up. We ordered the largest sundaes possible, figuring we would not pass this way again.

I had a good year, which helped ease the pain (but only slightly) of losing every night. I led the league in hitting with a, um, .620 batting average, and only years later did it occur to me that this may well have been because I was probably facing the weakest pitchers in the league because our team was so bad.

I learned to hit by reading a comic book that had a page of hitting tips from Stan the Man Musial.

Maybe I hit well because my father wasn't pressuring me to do well, standing along the fence by the dugout, shouting intructions and criticism like the other fathers always did.

"Really!" cried a chorus of voices in the bandshell.

Cus D'Amato, the famous boxing manager, once said to me that the key to Mike Tyson's success was that he didn't have a father around messing up his mind. Never thought of it that way. Thanks, Dad.

The class of the league every year was Kuhn's, a men's clothing store, which had the phenomenal Chuck Hutchcraft at shortstop. Were it not for Hutchcraft, my batting average would have been around .900. Hutchcraft was so good he made me cry. Literally, I'd drive balls to the left side—sure hits!—and Hutchcraft would vacuum them up and throw me out. I recall him doing it to me three times in a row, sending me back to the dugout sobbing: "He's too good, he's just too good. They shouldn't let him play!"

Kuhn's coach, Mr. Magnuson, was strange and ruthless. I came to dislike him when he coached the thirteen-to-fourteen-year-old team because I played the same position as his son, Keith, and his father never let me play. I sat on the bench the entire season and when he finally did put me in for an inning at third base I was nervous and blew my only chance. A line shot grounder was hit toward me at third—lightning fast. I stabbed at it and—wonder of wonders!—when I looked in my mitt, the ball was there. I fired it to second to start a double play. But alas, I threw it over second baseman Jimmy Peck's head into right field and, well, Mr. Magnuson only gave one chance to players unrelated to him who played the same position as his son. It was my last play in organized baseball.

"Sucks!" B.A. opined.

I couldn't really hit the curve ball. My physics teacher in high school said that curve balls don't really curve, that it is impossible to throw a ball that curves. I told him that they certainly do, and that if they didn't curve I'd be in the major leagues hitting well over .500. I didn't listen to another word he said all year.

The second-best team in our Texas League was usually Hayes Plumbing and Heating, with big Bill Bales on the mound. Bill Bales would not be allowed to play baseball today. I mean, forget lead-based paint and failure to use seatbelts and other leading causes of child mortality. The biggest threat to the health of children in East Central Illinois was Bill Bales On The Mound.

It's like: "Bill Bales On The Mound, Next *Donahue*!"

These two fingers are still somewhat disfigured from an errant Bill Bales fastball, a redundancy really, since all Bill Bales's pitches were fast and errant. The man—and he was too big at twelve to be considered a boy—would sometimes throw one *Over the Backstop!*

"Like Mean Gene!" came the chorus of my players.

Bales could hit like Mean Gene too. Once he smashed the windshield on a car that had nosed up to the outfield fence. Fans did that. This was the fifties, and they used to drive up to the fence and watch the games from their cars—honking when someone on their son's team did something good.

The kids looked a little perplexed by that one. Cars were more comfortable then, I explained.

"Were there any girls on your team?" Emily asked.

I don't think they had girls back then. Certainly not in Little League.

I'd start getting serious butterflies in my stomach about five o'clock on game days. When I was going to pitch, it was more like having condors in my stomach.

I loved playing third base. I was a pretty good fielder and I loved it when the ball would come hopping out to my left side so I could snatch it up on the move and fire it to first base in one smooth motion.

"Yeah!" said Neville, and I wondered how *he* could relate.

I loved the uniform, the chalked lines, the water dispenser in the dugout and the little Dixie cups. I liked the scoreboard and watching the kid putting up the numbers.

"Yeah!" said Hermie.

I liked being *out there,* on the diamond, *in the game,* with everyone watching—especially the girls. I always acted like I was way too absorbed in the game to notice them. But I did try to look as cool as possible while they were there. I always wished I were, you know, *bleeding* a little, or something to make the girls sympathetic.

I remember eating Dreamsicles after the games, that's about it. I don't have all that many sharp memories of that season. I think I try to block them out. Good training for Nam. If I ever do have a flashback it won't be about Nam. It will be about U of I Drugs, 1–17.

I went oh for two in the all-star game, and we didn't receive any of the trophies or plaques, ubiquitous today. Still, all was not lost. At the all-star game, they announced my batting average—good and loud—over a public address system, and the crowd went: Wuuuuuuuuuuuu!

I'll never forget that.

All the kids had been picked up but Monique.

"C'mon, Monique. Your mom won't be back for you 'til the mall closes at 9:00 P.M. I'll give you a ride."

"Thanks Mr. Geist, you're the greatest."

Wish she wouldn't say that.

STOOL CONCEPTS

There were games when I'd have to go snatch one of our players from his home at game time so we'd have enough players to avoid a forfeit, but they were all early for this one. Perhaps they smelled blood in the water in our makeup game with Yo Norb's Stool Concepts squad.

"Yo, Norb," I yelled. "Is Stool Concepts like a medical lab or what?"

"No," Norb explained, "it's a place out on the highway that sells barstools."

Wasn't sure you'd be willing to play today, Norb. Humidity's like 68 percent. Pretty high.

Virjean was in the stands holding forth on the dangers of wooden bats, having written a letter to the Commisioner of Major League Baseball regarding the bad example the majors set by still using wood.

Of course, wood bats are NOT highly dangerous, in my opinion, based on nearly four decades of playing baseball. But then I don't have a subscription to *Our Threatening World* magazine like she does.

Norb was the kind of coach who huddled all his kids together before the game, so they could put their hands together in the middle and yell: "One-two-three-deemphasize winning!" Damned near.

And Norb was successful in doing just that. His team was 0–5 on the season. We moved out to a 25–0 lead in the first three innings, and that was damned near all we played. Every time his players took the field, they all gathered at the pitcher's mound and held a sort of seventies-style "Love-In" therapy session during which Norb would ask the kids what positions they wanted to play. "How do you *feel* about playing catcher?" That sort of thing. Unfortunately they all say "Pitcher! Oh please, please, please!" Or "First Base! Oh please! Please! Pleeeeeease!"

Then Virjean would come out and explain to them why they all could not play the same position at the same time, so lovingly and caringly that you wanted to deck her. Paradoxically, after uncaringly running up a 25–0 lead, I could let my kids play anywhere they wanted. Want to pitch Monique? Now's your chance.

Anyway Norb's whole process took about fifteen minutes each inning, so when you played him, you could only get in about three innings before dark.

The single thing that slows Little League games the most is first convincing some kid that it's fun to play catcher—all that neat equipment!—and then getting the kid into all of that neat equipment, which not for nothing has been dubbed "the tools of ignorance."

It's a complicated procedure—each year they seem to add some new protective device to the medieval contraptions—throat guards and such. It takes a long time to get the stuff on, it hurts them a little when you pull the mask and helmet down over their ears, and no matter how much the league charges you to register your kid, the catcher's equipment is old, broken stuff.

After nine seasons of coaching, there's one thing I know: the guy who invents a one-piece protective suit for catchers that can be slipped on like coveralls in a few seconds *will be a millionaire.* It will reduce the time of Little League games by one-third.

Norbert was kind and caring toward his players, who nevertheless despised him for the "dork," "geek" and "nerd" that he certainly was.

"Yo Norb never wins!" Norb's pitcher confided in me over ice cream cones at Van Dyke's, where the teams hang out after the games. The pitcher said he was teased unmercifully about being humiliated every game.

I know, I said. I pitched on a team that went 1–17. But that was thirty years ago and I only think about it once or twice a day now.

Norbert took his teams to Van Dyke's win or lose, of course. So did I. Bill Shoulders, Knavery and Flint—all of the Pavlovian school of coaching—took their teams only when they won.

"Hey B.A.! Who said you could get a triple dip with sprinkles?!" Jesus. You take the team out for ice cream these days, it's thirty bucks. And they always sneak a brother or a friend in on you when you're not looking.

You eat the cones outside, and while I was standing there in the parking lot with rum raisin running down my forearm one of the parents on

Norb's team came up to tell me I was overemphasizing winning. She was unhappy about the 25–15 drubbing, of course. (Monique gave up a few runs.)

I explained to her that we'd done what we could to hold the score down, placing our best players in the outfield after the second inning at great risk of life and limb to those like Monique and Anand. She said that she appreciated my explanation, but would be taking the matter up with The Commissioner just the same—"nothing personal."

Hermie, Anand and Monique were the only players who had yet to get hits. For Anand and Monique, it looked like some sort of Divine Intervention would be necessary—something, Lord, on the order of The Bethlehem Thing.

Herm looked determined. At four feet six inches and about sixty pounds, he would step up and pound the plate with his bat before striking a rugged stance.

He beat on the plate nonstop until I yelled, "Hermie, here comes the ball!" Herm would look up, draw the bat back and swing as hard as he could. His strikeouts were monumental, and numerous, the rule rather than the exception. Everything else was a walk. Herm was not what you'd call a contact hitter, he was more of a. . . well, his coach last year would always yell "a walk's as good as a hit" and Hermie took it to heart. He didn't really swing anymore, he explained, because "when I do, bad things happen."

"The only thing holding me back is the equipment," he'd say. "The bats are too heavy."

Indeed we'd taught him just about everything we could think of. Batting is such a mind game.

My own son had what they call a "hitch" in his swing, which he picked up from imitating Dave Winfield. In hitting, as in so many things, TV is the enemy. The kids watch Wade Boggs or Rickey Henderson or Dave Winfield or Eric Davis and they imitate their unique styles. At the plate something subconscious goes on where they are so involved with trying to *look* like that person that they can't hit.

And after just a smidgeon of failure, some of the kids get it into their heads that they'll Never Again hit the ball. And, after all, major leaguers can't figure out how to get out of slumps. They try hypnotism, voodoo, "visualization," foot reflexology, wearing a different shirt—you name it.

Herm suggested getting Andy's chocolate-covered hands off the bat. Others (who were hitting) were actually starting to like the sticky chocolate on the handle.

I decided to invest in a lightweight bat for the team—one that Willie could use too. I went to Steep's Sporting Goods, where we had a charge account and were spending just over 50 percent of our family income: Food, 15 percent; Shelter, 25 percent; Clothing, 15 percent; and Athletic Shoes, 55 percent.

Basketball shoes are, like, one hundred dollars a pair and my son changes sizes every time he takes them off. He also "needs" baseball shoes, football shoes, soccer shoes, swimming shoes (yes!) and everyday sport shoes. My daughter needs them too. Nike Air, Reebok Pumps. My wife has tennis shoes and walking shoes. (Excuse me, but aren't *all* shoes walking shoes?) All of these shoes have more advanced engineering than the Stealth bomber. I once visited the Nike Labs in Oregon and witnessed the engineering testing that goes on. (Shouldn't all these guys in lab coats be discovering a cure for cancer or inventing the solar-powered automobile or something?) I also visited the factory in

Korea that makes all of the major brands—in the same factory!

All of this advanced engineering goes into developing shoes most people wear shuffling from the La-Z-Boy to the refrigerator.

I picked up the perfect bat for Herm: very, very light, and yet with an enormous barrel that provided a large target for the ball—and with Herm, that's how it was going to have to be, the ball looking for the bat like some bat-seeking missile.

I didn't care what it cost, this was just what I was looking for. The cashier was very friendly. "Good morning, Mr. Geist, how are you?" I took this less as a greeting than some attempt to gain inside information. If I wasn't feeling well, he might want to list the store with a commercial broker.

He rang up the bat. "Seventy dollars and nineteen cents," he said, avoiding eye contact. And of course in addition to that, I'd just tossed some extra-virgin yak-skin batting gloves on the counter: $19.95. Kids think this stuff makes you play well. That you can buy success. Very American.

"And while you're at it," I said, "throw in some wristbands. And maybe a pair of those forearm bands." *Got* to have forearm bands! Darryl Strawberry wears them. And he gets selected to the all-star team no matter how bad his batting average is!

And so it was that when Hermie stepped to the plate in the second inning of the game against Stool Concepts, I called time out and made a dramatic bid to reverse his fortunes.

I took my daughter's violin case to the plate and opened it to reveal: The Ultra-Lite, Boom-Barrel Natural Pro Balance LX1! Hallelujah! Hallelujah!

Now, to look at this bat you would have to say it was illegal. (They *are* illegal in softball, another issue hotly debated on the diamond.) Had to be. But, it was not. Rather this bat was a manifestation of our belief in the art of high technology and its ability to solve all of our problems—as applied here to leisure time activities. Someday, all men will hit .300. With Hermie, the future was now.

Herm's eyes brightened as I slipped on his wristbands and forearm bands. Then the rich (Corinthian, possibly?) yak-skin batting gloves.

When I handed him the bat I could almost hear the theme from *Rocky,* or was it *The Natural*? He pounded the plate. Watch it, Herm!

That's seventy bucks! He took two strikes—in the manner of Mighty Casey—before deciding to swing. "You gotta swing it yourself, Herm, batteries are not included!"

When he did, he swung mightily, and he made contact! He didn't exactly *hit* the ball, you understand, but he Made Contact, as they say, and the ball dribbled off to the left side as Hermie ran like a bat out of hell for first base. The pitcher, unprepared for this eventuality, fumbled the ball and Hermie was safe at first with the first hit of his life! Truly. It did not continue to work so well for Herm in future plate appearances. But what do you want for a hundred bucks? It was worth a hundred bucks to see Hermie's face as he stood on first base. The sick part is: I'm not kidding.

All the kids were supposed to play all the time, but Hermie kind of liked the bench, his domain. He owned the bench. Literally. In our upscale community with astronomically high property taxes, the sports facilities are meager, to say the least. Most of the fields not only have no place for the fans to sit, there are no dugouts and no benches—no place for the players to sit!

So, Hermie brought a bench for us to sit on. He

discovered it sitting on the curb on Big Trash Day, a major date on a suburbanite's calendar. It was a church pew, actually. He played the minimum required under criminal statutes—that's the only way they can get coaches to put guys like Hermie into the games, threaten them with long jail terms. Three to five. Only way you'd ever put Herm in.

"Why do I *have* to play?" he'd ask, straightening up the pile of bats, collecting used paper cups. Hermie was a housekeeper.

"There's a rule, you have to play two innings in the infield; supposed to play the whole game, Hermie."

"Why?"

"To have fun. You have to have fun. It's the law."

"I just want to be on the team, you know?"

So the problem was where to put him. "Can I play first base?" No way! Putting Hermie at first base would be tantamount to the ancient form of punishment known as stoning. He'd be completely defenseless at first base against oncoming baseballs. He certainly couldn't *catch* the damned things! He got to where he could *dodge*'em pretty well, which kept him alive all right, but sort of defeated the purpose, baseball-wise, of having him play the position. Better the ancient form of punishment known as banishment (to the outfield).

Herm took to managing the bench, keeping things in order. "Hey, put that bat back where you found it!" he'd snap.

He just struck out, Herm, he's upset.

"Yeah," his father would chuckle, "Hermie's a fastidious little bastard."

Herm was in charge of rally caps—turning hats around on our heads for luck when we were behind in the late innings. He'd clip pictures out of the newspapers of the Mets, who used to lead the league in inventive rally cap styles. And Hermie made sure everybody participated.

"Turn it around, B.A!" He'd say that stuff to Bad Ass McCarthy!

One day I brought Hermie a feather duster, as a joke. He took it and used it, keeping the bench tidy. Hermie was in absolute heaven when we won and went to Oakland, New Jersey, where they had real dugouts.

Hermie organized the bench, putting Andy in charge of yelling derogatory remarks aimed at the opposing team, or an opposing player.

Andy was loud, but was lacking in certain sensibilities, his favorite disparaging remark, and one that he used often, was a quick, rapid-fire: "Faggot!" and the closely akin: "Homo!" Then I'd have to say: "Andy, we can't have that." Especially not with Pat, Charlie's altogether effeminate father, sitting right behind us.

"Do you think Charlie's old man is a homo, Mr. Geist?" Andy asked one day before he arrived. I didn't know, but it was certainly an open topic of debate in the community.

"We don't say 'homo,' Andy," I corrected. "The preferred term is 'gay.' "

"Gee," said Andy, "he sure seems like a homo to me."

Andy was a bad boy, so it was his idea to start giving the "hotfoot" treatment to his teammates on the bench. But he wasn't quite smart enough to make the device necessary to give a hotfoot, and certainly not cagey enough to carry it off.

To give a player a hotfoot—the way it was done by Roger McDowell, then a relief pitcher on the Mets—one would wrap a couple dozen wooden matches together, tape them to the heel of someone's shoe, one match protruding as a fuse—and light it.

This, you do not get in the official Little League video, I can tell you.

The first time Andy and Herm teamed up to do it the victim was Neville, who was frightened half to death and who screamed and whose mother screamed at me—and my God, did The Commissioner hear about that! I had to suspend the two players for a game.

That was when Herm really got into being the concierge of the bench. He kept the bats neat and orderly, he picked up litter, he organized rally caps and informed mothers whose turn it was to bring water for the team to the next game. He even took up a collection from parents to buy ice cream for the team, and disbursed it . . . prudently.

Do we go for ice cream tonight? I'd ask.

"Not toniiiight," he'd reply.

BIG EARL'S LIQUOR CORRAL

Hey. Curl Up 'N' Dye was sporting a 3–1 record!

Now, in Little League your *team* can win, but as a coach you never do.

You can't win. You really can't. Even if you lose. Probably the safest way to avoid criticism as a Little League coach is to post a record somewhere around .500.

If you win, parents will say you are an over-driven Type-A (and we all now know what the A stands for), a killer, a monster, who Takes The Game Too Seriously. That was already beginning to happen at Game Five with Earl's Liquor Corral. Parents of players on the opposing team were . . .

muttering: "Too much emphasis on winning," "It's only a game," "These are just kids."

I'm sure. Three and one, in second place? Break up Curl Up 'N' Dye? Shut uuuup!

If you lose, other coaches will like you. Conversely, the kids on your team will say that you "suck." Their parents will grumble, saying this season just isn't any fun, that you have deemphasized winning so much that their children are losing a year in their development (presumably on the road to signing a contract with the Yankees), that their children are losing self-esteem and most likely will require psychoanalysis because of you!

If their children develop behavioral disorders at school, drop out, turn to drugs and begin knocking off 7-Elevens—they won't be surprised!

I once interviewed a high school football coach in Texas who lost his opening three games of the season and began wearing a bulletproof vest. And of course there was the case down there in which the mother of a would-be cheerleader hired a killer to bump off the mother of another would-be cheerleader—so the motherless girl would be too distraught to compete in cheerleader tryouts. Sure.

But all the nuts aren't in Texas. There was a

letter to the editor last year in one of our local suburban newspapers from a Little League baseball coach describing how the mother of one of his fourth-grader players sent the coach's son hate mail profanely criticizing the abilities of the coach's son and wishing the coach dead of a heart attack. The mother believed that the coach's son played too much and her son not enough. The fourth-grade baseball coach said he also received a bomb threat.

The pressure is not all from the parents, either.

The kids want to win. Let's say—out of the goodness of your heart (or, maybe The Commissioner attends the game)—you put a poor player at first base. As often as not the player himself will tell you to forget it, he isn't good enough, there's too much pressure on him, he'll blow the game and his teammates will hate him or laugh at him.

Still, the most serious problem facing the coach—and, perhaps the nation—is The Concerned Parent (censorship of Mark Twain in the classroom, seatbelts in shopping carts, you know.)

There are coaches who complain that parents just use Little League as a baby-sitting service.

This is true, but don't knock it. There's nothing worse than an angry mob of Concerned Parents hanging on the fence. And thank God for that fence! Lately, I've been thinking a little barbed wire on the top might not be a bad idea.

If you don't give all the kids an equal chance to play, the parents ride you. If you do give all the kids an equal chance to play, the parents . . . ride you: "You're giving the game away, for chrissake!" That's what B.A.'s dad was yelling at me during Game Five.

Parents will say: "Pardon me, I know you're the coach, and I really do hate to interfere in any way, but I was wondering, what kind of . . . an . . . asshole(!) plays his own kid ahead of my child, who is a lot better than your child?"

Parents who want to win will also say awful things about other players on the team, too—sometimes within earshot of the other players and their parents.

"You're putting *Hermie* in?" bellowed B.A.'s dad. "Why don't you just put Helen Keller out there for chrissake!"

Hermie's mother heard that. She'd shut him up. She turned and stared daggers. B.A.'s father glanced at her for an instant, not about to take back his remark, then turned back to the playing field: "C'mon, you guys!"

As mentioned, if you win a couple of games, people in town begin to talk about you as being some sort of vicious beast, possibly deranged, having something to prove, a prima facie cheater and generally a win-at-all-costs lowdown bastard. Of course when you coach their kids on an all-star team at the end of the season, they say you're just the kind of coach they want.

If you lose it's not that parents actually *hate* you so much as that they think you are . . . a mope. Or that you don't care enough, and that you're Spoiling It For The Kids. They aren't *learning* anything—as if the parents cared about learning. They really just want their kid to win and be happy. Don't we all?

"Why did he volunteer if he can't get the job done?" as B.A.'s father put it. That's another bad thing about winning: parents begin attending.

I had a minor player revolt on my hands midway through this game with Big Earl's Liquor Corral.

Jean, Lynne and Monique complained that they were sick and tired of playing the boring outfield. "It sucks," Jean explained. "Could you get anything for us in a trade?" Lynne asked helpfully. "No," I replied, failing to mention that you can't make trades. I felt like being a little cruel. Cruel but fair, that was my credo.

Gee, and it was just beginning to look like we might have a winning season, too.

"It's the coach's responsibility," said Jean's mother, "to challenge each child and allow him or her to have a broadening recreational experience." Ay-yi-yi.

I put Jean at first, hoping against hope that it wouldn't be her nose that was broadened. I counseled Willie and the others not to throw the ball too hard. In fact, if you have time to run it over and tag the bag yourself. . .

I put Lynne at second base, Emily at third, Hermie at shortstop, and B.A. on the bench.

With this, B.A.'s father got up, snapped closed his folding chair, grabbed B.A.'s arm and said "Let's go!" He dragged B.A. off, they got in the car and had a terrific argument.

We were ahead 11—zip, and I figured with the rule that no member of a team can bat twice in the same inning, the most runs they could even possibly score would be twelve. They did.

Andy's father came over and asked: "Are you f——ing nuts? Putting those girls in the infield?" Andy's father smelled like he had been in the bar car on the commuter train. "Say," I said, "could you bring your breath over this weekend? I'm stripping some furniture."

"Funny, numb nuts," he said. "You're four and one. You got a shot at the championship. Or did, 'til today!"

Jean's mother came over and accused me of endangering the health of her daughter by forcing her to play first base.

"But she pleaded with me to play first base," I said.

"Do you really believe that a ten-year-old child knows what's best for her?" Jean's mother replied angrily. "I pity your children!"

Nothing can prepare you for how you will act at your child's Little League games.

There may be dark sides to your personality that you did not know existed; reservoirs of bile; things that twenty-five thousand dollars' worth of psychoanalysis has not brought out. But Little League will.

All will be revealed—tonight!

I have bad games and good games, doctor. Sometimes I am the picture of the good sport, complimenting the other team's good plays, being laid back. I think medicine would help.

"And you've got my kid batting ninth in the lineup?" asks Jean's father. "What kind of a message is that? Her self-esteem average is probably about zero-zero-zero right now, pal. You haven't even given her a chance! Ever hear of a little human kindness, idiot?!"

Of course, I feel the same way when I'm a parent in the stands. Oh sure! Play your kid at first base and leave my kid on the bench. My child is looking at me forlornly and there's nothing I can do.

It could be worse. The ten-year-old child of a friend of mine is on an all-star soccer team that travels to places like North Carolina where the kid sits on the bench.

I can humiliate my friends and family with the best of ' em. I yell at umpires and referees. It's an authority thing. Show me a guy in a uniform and I'll yell at him.

"Maybe if you'd stop yelling and offer some of your time to help out, we'd have better coaches and umpires," suggested a kindly man, challenging my right to yell at an umpire during one of Willie's games. I informed him that I had offered thousands of hours of my help and the umpiring was still atrocious! Later, I would discover that I was railing at the principal of the school my son would be attending next year. Super.

You may cheer too loudly when your team is winning, to get back at that Awful Parent who is rooting for the other team and applauding when your child drops the ball.

You may find yourself accusing a perfectly fine man coaching the other team of being a cheater. Don't be surprised.

This will carry over into other areas. I am best known for yelling at state troopers and basketball referees. I have never been thrown out of a gym—other fathers have!—but I did draw a technical foul once in Neptune, New Jersey, from a septua (at best) genarian referee who couldn't run up and down the court, so he called fouls while standing stationary at one end of the court. And seemingly at random.

In the town next to ours there are parents who act up so badly that they are banned from attending games. The year before my son began his Little League career—at the very same field—police had been summoned to break up a brawl between two parents.

Are these people crazy?

Yes. Temporarily insane. LLS.

A lot of fathers think that you, as the coach or umpire, are the only obstacle standing between their son and the New York Yankees. But get this! Some of the very worst parents I've ever encountered have been at girls' softball games.

At one of my daughter's softball games, a couple who apparently thought we were cheating (by not playing each kid in the infield two innings) began yelling obscenities at me. They started their team chanting "Libby stinks! Libby stinks!" at my ten-year-old daughter.

Kids are much more mature than adults. Libby

smiled. She knew that she most certainly does not stink and saw this for what it was: a compliment, really, that she was singled out for chiding.

I stifled an impulse to shove my lineup card down the parent's throat, instead walking over and showing him my legal pad with the name of every kid and which position the kid was playing in each inning. "Obviously," he said loudly, "you have mistaken me for somebody who gives a (bleep)!" Was it Confucius who said that or a T-shirt I saw at the Jersey Shore?

Anyway, it turns out that this was all his way of venting a season of frustration at winding up on Yo Norb's team and losing every game. The real problem was that I didn't get the man's name, and I wound up drafting his daughter on my next basketball team.

On occasion parents are very, *very* bad and sue a coach for more playing time for their child. Truly! It happened in a suburb nearby.

I prefer the kindred spirits who bitch about having to eat dinner at 4:30 in the afternoon so the kids can be at pregame practice, parents for whom Little League is something to be endured, like root canal work. They complain, as well they should, of boredom, of being struck by foul balls and of rheumatoid arthritis from sitting on the cold, damp ground.

With two outs in the bottom of the sixth inning against Big Earl's Liquor Corral, we were behind 20–19, when Willie hit the ball and Neville scored the tying run, or so we thought.

A parent on the other team jumped up and said Willie had overrun second base and was tagged out before Neville scored. No one else saw it. The umpire admitted he hadn't. But Dragonetti must have thought—"yeah, that's the ticket, the guy was tagged out at second for the third out and we win the game." Sure. Dragonetti decided he had seen it too. I maintained the umpire had to call people out, not some parent on the sidelines. "Hey," Dragonetti said to me, "we have to play by the honor system. We have to trust each other." As repugnant an idea as that was—trusting Dragonetti! How many men had *died* turning their backs on Dragonetti?!—I had to agree with him in principle. We lost the game. I had given it to them. However you want to look at it. Most members of my team cried, while the Liquor Corral team whooped it up. Meeks said he also thought maybe Willie was out. B.A. and Andy dumped the contents of the water cooler on him.

VICTORIA'S SECRET

Next, we were supposed to go up against Dick Knavery and his undefeated ChemLawn squad. Their official record was 4–1. They'd won all of their games, but forfeited one after Tony Dragonetti took exception to Knavery's slipping a twelve-year-old "cousin" from out of town into his lineup.

Thursday night and all week long the kids had been harassing each other at school. As for me, I'd again been carrying an extra legal pad around all week, hauling it out during business meetings and scrawling down different combinations of players and different batting orders to try and come up with something formidable. Formidable? I always came to the same conclusion: I was going to have to have Monique and Anand rubbed out.

This would be the biggest game of the year for us thus far, weather permitting. It was not permitting. Thursday dawned cold and rainy and stayed that way.

This game would not be rescheduled. I didn't want to play Knavery's team, and he certainly didn't want to risk his first place by playing mine. But there would be another chance, at the end of the season.

We all looked forward to the next game, because it was against Victoria's Secret Wildkits. The kids looked forward to the game because the Wildkits were 1–5 on the season. I looked forward to it, because it was Jack Caper's team.

"Hi Jack," I said, looking along the fence. "Quite a lineup this year."

Indeed:

—At mother of the pitcher: Angela Dominico, perhaps the best-looking woman in the county. Long thick dark brown hair, pouting Bardot face, "stacked" (if I may) and given to wearing out-and-out Slutwear: ultra-tight, ultra-short skirts, blouses with perhaps one button at the navel, spike heels. Thought to be the best all-around mother in the draft this year.

—Mother of the shortstop: perhaps the most improved mother in the draft, following liposuction and breast augmentation in the off-season.

—Mother of the left fielder: a woman of tremendous stature in the community—probably on the order of 42-28-38, oddsmakers say. A natural.

—Definitely the Rookie of the Year: a twenty-three-year-old airline stewardess, who had adopted a ten-year-old child.

"One question, Jack. How do we get invited to your team party at the end of the season?"

With our team leading 6–0 in the first inning, play was stopped—not officially, but in reverence—for the entrance of Angela Dominico, arriving fashionably late in a painfully tight-fitting sleeveless blouse, crotch-crimping gold lamé capri pants, designer sunglasses and a baseball cap with rhinestones.

"Wow!" someone said. I turned around to see who'd said it. B.A.

"You're only ten years old, B.A. . . . Pitch."

I waved at Angela. I applauded enthusiastically when her Joey did . . . anything.

I couldn't *wait* until our next game with Caper's team, the last week of the season, when the weather would be warm and there would be no telling how scanty the outfits would be. Capers' team always drew large crowds at the end of the season. Camera day.

HALFWAY HOME

Midseason. Time to take stock. Knavery's ChemLawn team was in first place, and our team, Curl Up 'N' Dye, was in the thick of it, in second place, somehow.

1. ChemLawn, 5–1
2. Curl Up 'N' Dye, 4–2
3. Discreet Pest Control, 4–3
4. Earl's Liquor Corral, 3–3
5. Jiffy Lube, 3–3
6. Ridgewood Corset Shop, 3–4
7. Victoria's Secret, 3–4
8. Stool Concepts 0–7

♦ ♦ ♦

It was looking like we'd have to win all of our games in the second half of the season if we were to keep up with Knavery. If he hadn't forfeited he'd be undefeated. Of course, if he weren't a cheat he wouldn't have had to forfeit; and come to think of it if he weren't a cheat he might not have won a game all year. Might not have an $800,000 home.

The task for our team was made all the greater in light of the recent trade. Trades are prohibited, but Knavery convinced one of his girls—his number *thirteen* batter, as it happened—that she would be much happier playing with her best friend on Norb's team, and that Norb's number *four* hitter (cleanup) had a good *friend* on Knavery's team so they should switch.

The fact that the number four hitter had never *met* anyone on Knavery's team was incidental, but Knavery just knew that she'd be best friends with all of them if only she had a chance to meet them.

Of course Knavery was taking a chance; the number four hitter on Norb's team might not be as good as the number thirteen hitter on his team. Norb coached in mysterious ways.

Anyway, it all made sense to Norb—yup! yup! yup!—and Barney: "Whatever's best for the children." Whose children?

Emily was a gem, an unexpected treasure. Danny was gone, and good riddance! Willie was doing well, Byron lead the league in home runs, Charlie was having a good season (much to Knavery's chagrin), Andy had real power (but could still be thrown out at first base from the outfield as he chugged along), Lynne was heavyset and every so often got her weight behind one.

Jean was a pleasant surprise. Her batting average must have been about .900. She hit the ball every time, and every time it went about five feet, making it, in effect, a bunt (which is illegal in this league), but they had to allow it because she was swinging as hard as she could. Neither pitcher nor catcher can get to the baseball and throw her out. By all rights Jean should probably be the lead-off hitter, but I was so enjoying watching Emily demoralize the opposition in the leadoff spot.

Neville's father was still in office. Neville had developed a quirk of getting two strikes and going back to the bench and sitting down. "Get back in the batter's box, Neville!" his father would shout. "Back in the box!"

Hermie had the one hit, and Anand and Monique were looking a bit more pathetic with each passing game.

I was trying to teach Anand to just stand there and try to draw a walk once in a while, instead of swinging feebly at bad pitches (and, for that matter, good pitches!).

"You know, Anand, if the pitch is a ball . . . you don't have to swing."

"Is not pitch always ball?"

"Well in that sense, yes, it's always a baseball that is pitched. But if it's way up here or down here, don't swing. A walk's as good as a hit."

"Sometimes," he replies, "you tell us it is good to walk. Other times you say we must run as fast as we can. I don't know why."

I watch Anand bat, and all I can think of is that maybe he refuses to hit the ball on *religious* grounds or something—cowhide and all that. "I think the ball is horsehide, Anand." Same reason he bought that polypropylene baseball glove at K-Mart. Cowhide. Reverence for cows. You know.

With Monique, my strategy was to ask her as

often as I could without making her cry: "Having *fun,* Monique? Do you *like* baseball? There are so many *other* fun things to do in springtime. Spring soccer, lacrosse, swimming at the Y and, you know what's really fun on Saturdays? Going shopping at the mall! Do you *like* shopping, Monique? Sure you do. But with baseball, who has the time?"

"No, Mr. Geist, I like baseball just fine. And you're the best coach I've ever had."

Aaargh.

We had a player added to our team at midseason, because there is a waiting list and because Danny had gone over the wall.

Foozle called. "We have a boy here named Marcel."

Sounded like a pastry chef to me, but he turned out to be a good little ballplayer.

Meeks, my assistant coach, quit. Said he didn't have the time. Finally admitted he didn't have the stomach for it either. "All of the conniving, the bitterness. These are kids. It's just a game. Winning isn't important." I always knew he had a bad attitude.

♦ ♦ ♦

"Children, mental patients and prisoners may not have an effective option when officials declare game time"—Erving Goffman.

Midseason is also a time for reflection. I mean: do you think Little League baseball is an explication of baseball's symbolism as a ritual exemplification of the Freudian primal horde scenario (Petty, 1967), or is it just a youth activity that all too often "really sucks" (Bad Ass McCarthy, 1991).

Sometimes, when one coach is calling another one—ohh, let's see, the term "shithead" was being bandied about at yesterday's game—I think: Forgive Carl, Lord, for he knew not what he did.

I refer, of course, to Carl Stotz, who founded Little League baseball in Williamsport, Pennsylvania, in 1939—with the help of the Bebble boys—George and Bert. It has grown from a three-team league to become what the *New York Times* called "an indelible part of America's cultural and institutional landscape"—like it or not. It has become an international enterprise with assets of more than $10 million and seven thousand leagues in thirty-seven countries—having recently expanded to Yugoslavia and Czechoslovakia. More than 2.5 million boys (and a few girls) aged six to eighteen take part.

Little League boasts that 750,000 adult volunteers help out—and some say that if they could just somehow convince that 750,000 to stay home everything would be fine. Carl Stotz thought that adult supervision would eliminate bickering!

The home office also boasts such esteemed graduates of the program as Vice-President Dan Quayle (who, perhaps not surprisingly, played on a team sponsored by his father); Kareem Abdul-Jabbar and Danny DeVito (of wildly varying strike zones), singer Bruce Springsteen and—of course—myself. It is one of a handful of organizations in this country chartered by Congress.

Little League became big business fast and Mr. Stotz was forced out of his leadership role by court order in 1955. U.S. Rubber, which had taken over the league, forced him out, and the local sheriff's office had to guard the doors. Stotz called the league he founded "a Frankenstein" because of its new commercialism.

George Bebble doesn't care for the game much anymore, having made uncharitable remarks about the excessive seriousness of the whole thing as well as about Mr. Stotz, who Bebble says often forgets to mention the Bebble boys as founders of the league along with him.

Indeed, George Bebble fought a proposal a couple of years ago by the mayor of Williamsport to erect a statue of Stotz, whose home is a kind of annex to the official Little League Museum.

In the beginning, the founders contacted fifty-eight firms for funds, unsuccessfully, until Floyd A. Mutchler of Lycoming Dairy Farms shelled out some money and uttered those immortal words: "We'll go along with the boys."

The legend of Little League baseball begins in 1938 in Williamsport, Pennsylvania, in Stotz's backyard, where he was playing catch with two nephews aged six and eight, Harold and Jimmy Gehron.

They thought up the idea of a league, and a week or so later Stotz packed up the two nephews and about ten friends in his 1934 Plymouth and drove to a field, which became the birthplace of Little League baseball.

How different that first game was from those we see today. One adult, no coaches, no parents watching, no organizing committees, no sponsors, no corporation, no bylaws, no volumes of rules, no standings.

Using folded newspapers as bases, Stotz and the boys played the first game. Occasionally, as the story goes, Stotz would adjust the distance between the bases, and the distance from the pitcher's mound to home plate, until they seemed right for young boys: sixty feet between bases rather than the ninety in the big leagues, and forty-six feet from the pitcher's mound to home plate rather than sixty feet six inches.

The inaugural season was 1939, with but three teams. The first league winner was the Lycoming Dairy Farms team, which included the Gehron brothers.

By 1947, when the first Little League World Series was played, there were sixty teams playing in fifteen leagues in two states. U.S. Rubber underwrote the 1948 series, paying traveling expenses, and team players wore U.S. Pro Keds. Two years later there were 867 teams in 197 leagues in twelve states. U.S. Rubber assumed all expenses for the national headquarters and gave Stotz a salary and a paid assistant.

With the baby boom, Little League took off. Its status changed from nonprofit to for-profit, and Peter J. McGovern, PR director for U.S. Rubber in Detroit, began a thirty-one-year term of managing the league. Stotz was out.

The museum is festooned with all manner of banners and homilies: the voice of Dale Murphy admonishing young players to catch the ball with both hands and squeeze it in the glove, which is pretty much what I tell them—"Two hands, meathead!" The batting cages—complete with videotape replays of your swing—are often usurped by adults.

The complex comprises forty-two acres in Williamsport, with the museum, five diamonds, the batting cages, housing for summer baseball campers, corporate offices, and famous Lamade Stadium, home of the Little League World Series—televised by ABC with a very healthy fifteen share last year.

Little League Baseball, Inc., brags in its promotional materials that it's "training for life." That's what they tell you in the army, too, until you go out and go job hunting for a career in tank repair.

In the opinion of those at the top, Little League is more than baseball, of course, it's the building of stoic citizens. That's a tall order for a little game you play several times a year, but they think it does even more than that! They claim it provides kids with a sense of competition, responsibility, teamwork and reward. In short: it embodies all that society holds dear.

Not all agree. Critics think it's too competitive, too serious, no fun. It has been pointed out by a University of Washington sports psychologist that one of the real problems of youth sports is that "we erroneously apply a professional model to a developmental situation."

"Do they have to learn all the Hard Truths at age eight, nine and ten?" I asked Bud Flint, over a beer after a game a couple of years ago. He was arguing that less talented kids should be cut from the teams. I said that his position seemed to be that every kid should be in an airline crash to get an idea of just how difficult life can really be.

At the risk of sounding like some Barney Foozle disciple, I told Flint that he made the game too much like work, with his constant yelling for them to "work harder out there"—always the rhetoric of the workplace. He seemed worried that it could degenerate into . . . fun.

We debated whether Little League passed along an unhealthy sense of competition. "Don't knock it," Flint said. "It's what made this country what it is today." We shook on that.

Dateline: Chicago—A three-year study of Little League baseball published by the University of Chicago Press concludes: "Basically, Little League is fun for those preadolescents who participate, and while we should never stop trying to curtail its flaws, we should be satisfied that it brings a little joy to the lives of our children." Three years, and that's it?!

THE BIG GAME

In the second half of the season, Knavery's team kept on winning in quasilegal fashion, and held a 10–1 record with just one major hurdle between it and the Ridgewood World Series. Us. We were, somehow, 9–2. If we beat his ChemLawn team we'd have identical records but our victory over them would put us in the Series.

So the whole season came down to this. One game. Nerves were on edge. Thank God for Royce.

Royce is Jean's father. I had already decided to vote him into *my* Little League Hall of Fame (Parental Wing), because in recent days he had taken to bringing a thermos to the games filled with chardonnay.

"Hot one today, isn't it?" Royce said when he

saw me. "A man could work up a powerful thirst after a spell on a dusty diamond."

I knocked back a little Dixie cup full, before going over to face Coach Knavery to exchange lineups.

I was worried about what Knavery might have up his sleeve. He might ferret out some obscure subsection of the rules to seal his victory before the game began.

Before a big game last year, he dug up some corollary from some dusty old rule book which mildly suggested that his best pitcher was exempt from the maximum-innings-pitched-per-week rule because it was a makeup game. And he had presented a legal brief to Foozle in support of his position. The very *thickness* of it was enough to decide the case.

"Oh yeah," my daughter remarked, "Joe Jeffries, a kid in my class, does the same thing. He triple spaces his book reports and puts them inside one of those five-dollar plastic covers."

Knavery didn't miss a trick. His own children were bright kids whom he'd held back a year in school to make them look like geniuses and world-class athletes when up against kids a year younger. The concept has caught on to the point where our kindergartners now receive first-grade instruction.

In Cub Scouts, Little Dick won the Pinewood Derby—a race of little balsa wood model cars down a ramp—every year because Big Dick had the boy's car made in the engineering lab of the company he worked for. Kid never touched the car.

"Dick, how ya doin'?" I said, greeting him with *genuinely* false congeniality. You always met Dick at home plate, a neutral area. The DMZ. You always felt that if you so much as set foot on his side of the diamond, his co-coach for security would open up on you with a .50-caliber machine gun mounted in a nearby tree.

"Boy, I'll tell you (heh-heh)," I continued in my best folksy manner, "I hope we get nine kids to show up." Of course, I *knew* all twelve were dressed and chomping at the bit, but everybody does a little sandbagging before Little League games.

"I doubt you'll need nine," Dick countered. "My pitcher's been sick all week."

"Gee," I said, "that's too bad, Dick, I hope it's

nothing serious." That's what I said. What I was thinking, was: "Blow it out your ass, Dick."

His pitcher, Mean Gene Huffman, was warming up on the sidelines, looking more than ambulatory, throwing seventy-mile-an-hour fastballs. It was Dick himself who didn't look so hot. The word was that Dick gets so churned up on game days that he contracts flulike symptoms of the lower intestinal tract.

Well, he must have been wearing Depends for this game. This one was as big as they get. Everybody knew it. The winner would move on to the exalted World Series of Ridgewood to play the best team from the east side of town.

But this game seemed somehow even more important than the series itself because this one was in the neighborhood, played against players and coaches who would remind you—either by never shutting up about it or by their mere presence—for the Rest of Your Life that *you lost.*

Or you would remind them that *you won.*

Almost all parents were there. Grandparents. Brothers, sisters. Kids. The other coaches and players from the other teams. Yes, even Commissioner Barney Foozle was in attendance.

Sportsmanship took a holiday. There is a rule that coaches had to start their batting order in the current game right where it left off at the end of the last one. That is, if your eleventh batter made the last out in the previous game, your number twelve batter—your worst batter—would lead off in the next game.

That is: Anand made the last out in the last game (Surprise!), so, rightfully, Monique would be the leadoff hitter in this game. But, do you actually *believe* I would even *consider* doing that in a game as important as this? Get serious.

Nope, Emily would lead off in this most important game of the season.

And guess what? As fate would have it, the leadoff hitter on Knavery's team was leading off this game too! Neither of us said anything. Honor among thieves.

This was Take No Prisoners, Scorched-Earth Little League Baseball.

As we wrote down each other's lineup in our score books, I commented: "Just ten players today, Dick?"

His *best* ten.

"I'm missing a few," Bob said. "Some sort of flu going around."

"Yeah," I replied. "They say a virus always attacks the weakest first."

The weakest hitters! The son-of-a-bitch had probably told his weakest players that this game was *tomorrow*! He'd done it before.

I had all twelve, as usual. Great to see that kind of enthusiasm.

Knavery's team was warming up. In batting practice, Mean Gene was blasting the ball out to the fence and beyond as my players stood there in awe.

"We're dead," Neville commented.

"Shut up," I replied. "Break it up," I said. "Go throw the ball around."

How I had longed this past week to see Mean Gene's picture on a milk carton.

Then we had the field for practice. I hit the ball to Charlie, who scooped it up and threw it to Willie. Byron and Andy did the same. Emily, too. Some of the others were even getting the hang of it. "Nice throw, Neville."

I hit it hard to Willie. I always asked more of him. Not fair. He fielded it and stepped on first. Had to be the best fielder in town. The kind of kid who annoyed the hell out of opposing coaches. You pray for your kids to just hit the ball, and then . . . there's some kid like Willie who puts them out one after the other all game long. The Terminator.

Caper had a first baseman like that. Little bastard. I was coaching first base one inning when the kid made two sensational putouts in a row, and I stepped forth and dramatically offered the kid a five-dollar bill to stop it. Do you think The Commissioner's Office heard about *that* one?

At the other end of the spectrum, we had Monique, who *still* at the end of the season would not "Get in Front of the Ball!" nor "Get Your Glove Down!"

She was a little late in arriving, and naturally I was concerned—concerned she'd show up after all.

I knew it was wrong to actually *pray* for something like this, but I did look briefly to the heavens in muttering, "Don't let it be anything toooo terrible, just please don't let her make it to this game." Alive.

But! There's our little sweetheart. Right before game time—too late to warm up or anything (she never came to practice)—her mom ejected her from the car and sped away.

At the office that day I had gone over and over possible fielding combinations that would not just . . . give the damned game away . . . when we had to bring our weaker players into the infield. You could alleviate the suffering a bit. Let's say Anand was at third base, you could put B.A. in short, short, short left field, say *three feet* behind him. That sort of thing.

We were the underdog, but something of a crowd favorite, Dick Knavery being the Saddam Hussein of Ridgewood baseball.

A few of the other coaches came over and wished me well, their sentiments perhaps best summed up by Tony Dragonetti: "Beat this prick!"

There was something surprisingly sentimental about those three little words, believe it or not, coming from a man who most of the time regarded me as something of a prick myself. But you don't have to swim at the Y to know that pricks come in a variety of sizes.

In our league, you are really supposed to let kids coach the bases, certainly by this point in the season. Not in The Big Game. Fathers would coach the bases in this one. And not just any fathers. Red meat-eaters who drove pickup trucks or BMWs. Not the father who wore Birkenstock sandals.

Base coaching is a big part of Little League baseball. Competitive fathers who coach bases scream at the players. Sometimes they take hold of the left arm of a runner to hold him on base until it's safe to advance, then literally shove the runner toward the next base. Sometimes they shove so hard the base runners fall down. Dick's third base coach this day is a man known for holding the kids so tightly they get black and blue pinch marks on their biceps. Or he'll swat them on the butt and yell "Score! Score! Score!" I've been known to do it myself, but you could always tell a kid on Knavery's team by the bruises on the upper arms.

Can a kid actually be six feet five inches tall when he's ten years old? Well that's how big Mean Gene looked on the mound. In truth he was a mere five feet eight inches—huge—out there firing the ball as hard as he could. And closing his eyes at the last moment! Aieee!

You could always tell players who had recently *played* Knavery's team, as well, by the Mean Gene–related bruises on their left sides. Some wore slings.

Pitchers in our league are only allowed to pitch

six innings per week, but it was widely believed Mean Gene had pitched every inning for the past two months.

"Plenty of ice packs on hand, Hermie?"

"Check, coach."

"Play ball!" yelled the umpire. We had a "real" ump for this game—a high school senior. Sometimes the umps don't show up and parents have to umpire.

Never Do This.

Do Not Umpire. Everyone will hate you. If you give your child a break at the plate, the other team, parents of the other team, and the other coach will all hate you. Both coaches will wind up disliking you in any case. If you go so far as to be objective—actually calling them as you see them—you actually put yourself in the position of calling your own child out on strikes. Your own child will hate you. Forever. Remember, child psychologists charge a hundred bucks an hour. And you'll be needing one too.

In the top of the first inning, with B.A. on the mound for us, Knavery's team scored three runs, Mean Gene driving in all three runs with a triple.

Oh, here's *another* annoying thing about Knavery: every time one of his players does something good, *he* tries to take credit for it.

Have you seen this? With Gene standing on third base, smiling proudly, Knavery tries to steal the show: "You see what I told you, Gene? See what happens when you step toward the pitcher when you swing?"

Gene gets a blank look on his face. He is confused, probably because Knavery has never told him to step toward the pitcher when he swings. Not to mention: Mean Gene Huffman could hit triples in utero, long before he ever *met* Knavery. Presumably, at this point all the parents are supposed to be thinking: "He owes it all to Knavery, a great coach, and a fine human being." We *do* know this: that's what *Knavery's* thinking!

But not all parents are thinking that. I am a parent. I am thinking: Dick Knavery is an asshole.

The challenge in the bottom of the first was to make our players actually go to the plate to face Mean Gene. Emily did. Awestruck by the blazing speed, she stood there . . . and walked.

Charlie followed suit. "Good eye! Make it be your

pitch,'' I yelled, hoping to make myself clear: don't even *try* to hit the ball. *Pray* for a walk. It's your only hope.

Willie was—ohh God!—hit by a pitched ball. Fortunately it bounced in front of the plate first before it struck him.

"Herm!" I yelled, and he ran out with the first-aid kit, applied the Quik Ice, and the game resumed.

Now the bases were loaded, and Mean Gene could throw just as hard and as wildly as he wished, given the local rule that runs could not be walked in.

Even B.A. had fear in his eyes now. I saw his mother turn away. And none too soon. The first pitch nailed him right in the back as he turned away to protect himself.

"Medic!" I yelled, and Herm ran out again. I could tell Herm was liking this, the twisted little cuss. A tear ran down B.A.'s face. I felt sorry for him and at the same time knew I could not let our other players see B.A.—Bad Ass!—crying, or the whole team would be demoralized.

I told B.A. that his was a noble gesture, that in baseball parlance this was known as "taking one for the team," which means getting hit more or less on purpose to get on base and, in this case, force in a run.

Three to one.

Andy struck out swinging as did Marcel. Against overpowering pitchers like Gene, the poorer hitters often do better than the good ones because they don't make the mistake of thinking they can actually hit the ball.

Now we had a problem. Neville was up next and he believed that he really did not wish to go to the plate to bat against Mean Gene.

"I'll go if you won't," Lynne said. Neville went to bat. In a sense. He took up a batting position several yards from the plate itself, to stay out of harm's way. Not ideal for hitting, certainly, but safer.

Hey, what do you want from kids who have grown up in car safety seats and bicycle helmets? We have convinced a generation of kids—haven't we, Virjean?—that they live in a threatening world in which most of life is not to be experienced but avoided. And in the suburbs, batting against Mean Gene is about as threatening as life will *ever* be.

The umpire did not look kindly on this rather uncompetitive approach to hitting, however. He kind of enlarged the strike zone for Gene, and Neville struck out.

In the top of the second inning, B.A. took the mound and tried to prove he could throw as hard as Gene. He walked the first three batters, then Gene came to the plate. Gene often hit home runs by accident. On the first pitch, the ball came right for Gene's head. Gene hit the dirt.

Knavery charged out of the dugout, yelling at me. "He did that on purpose! Your pitcher threw the ball at my player on purpose!"

"He did no such thing!" I yelled. I mean, the nerve! Suggesting something like that.

I strolled out to the mound. "Just calm down, B.A.," I said. "I know you didn't throw at Gene on purpose, did you?"

"F——in' A," he replied.

"Don't do it again," I counseled, "not for a while."

Gene tripled again. Lynne made a great throw from center to save a home run. I tried to remain positive. "Great throw, Lynne!" I was starting to feel calm and good-natured, which could only mean one thing: the game was getting beyond our reach, to the point where I could almost become a good sport.

Six to one.

♦ ♦ ♦

We didn't score anymore for . . . hours . . . it seemed.

B.A. was pitching well, so I left him in for the entire game. Also, members of Dick's squad had taken to hurling ethnic slurs and racial epithets at the foreign-born on my roster, so I really didn't want to put Emily on the mound.

By the top of the sixth we were behind 12–4, and dusk was falling. The parents of my players were all gathered around Royce and—thanks be to the thermos—taking the loss with remarkable equanimity.

Knavery tried to have the game called on account of darkness, but the umpire noted that the nearest street light had not come on. That was the rule. I had to admit it was getting rather dark, but Who Are We to second-guess light-sensor technology?

B.A. struck out two in the top of the sixth, but ChemLawn threatened to blow it wide open—as they say—when Mean Gene stepped to the plate with the bases loaded and rocketed a line drive to left field. Right at Jean, who didn't have time to get out of the way and stuck her little glove up in front of her face for protection. This may sound like her obituary in tomorrow's paper but—miraculously—the ball hit her glove, nearly tearing it from her hand, and stuck in the webbing.

She'd caught the ball! Everyone just stood there in shock, eyewitnesses to a miracle. Then we went wild. Something to cheer about.

Knavery stalled, waiting for it to become pitch dark out there. "What the hell's wrong with the street light?" he roared after the umpire told him to hurry up getting the equipment on his catcher. I removed my glasses for a second to see if perhaps I still had on my sunglasses. I did not.

Charlie came to bat first in the bottom of the sixth and final inning and, in the gathering darkness, struck out. Willie was next up, and having been hit by Mean Gene in two of his last three trips to the plate, pleaded: "Gene, pleeease don't hit me again! Pleease." Gene was touched by this, by the fact that he was hurting his friends. For a killer, he was a pretty nice guy. But then: isn't that what the neighbors always say about mass murderers?

Willie and Mean always played on the same basketball teams. My teams. The other coaches, like Flint, wouldn't take him in the draft because they thought he had "an attitude problem." I would always pipe up: "I'll take that (five-foot-eight-inch) attitude problem," and we'd always win the league title.

After nine years of coaching, I have concluded: Coaches Who Talk About Kids Having Attitude Problems Usually Have Attitude Problems. "Sorry, Will," Gene said, and he began throwing slowly so he could get more accuracy and not maim his friends.

"Gene, whataya doin'? Fire that ball!" Knavery yelled.

Willie looked at two slow strikes before he caught on. Then, he hit the next pitch farther than any ball he'd ever hit before, onto the hood of a gray Volvo wagon in the street for a home run. The fans erupted: Was that *your* gray Volvo wagon? No, was it your gray Volvo wagon? No, was it yours . . .

It was the beginning of a rally, which was making us feel a whole lot better about things even if we weren't going to win.

I had to take a little of the credit for this. Well, I don't have to, but: We're All a Little Knavery to Some Degree.

Ice Cream Revitalization Therapy. After some of our best hitters had struck out in the previous two innings, I inquired: "What the hell's with you guys? B.A.? Charlie? You guys don't strike out!"

I found out that Andy held a "sleepover" the night before—an absolute misnomer—attended by Charlie, B.A. and some others, and that (by definition) none of them slept. This violated a hard and fast rule of mine that none of the kids ever listened to: No Sleepovers Before a Big Game.

I took emergency action. This being a big game, the Mister Whippee ice cream truck was there, so I dispatched my wife, Jody, to buy thirteen chocolate-covered ice cream bars. Sugar!

Hyperactivity? Insulin Shock? Who cares? We needed some instant energy, and we got it. Oh yes, another thing for coaches to remember: Sugar Works.

When the rally started, I sent Jody back to buy Monique a Super Quencher soft drink, one of those that comes in a garbage-can-sized plastic container. More on that in a moment.

B.A. tripled off another slow pitch from a kinder, gentler Gene. Andy drove him in with a double. Herm set Neville's shoe on fire. Foozle scowled. Knavery fumed.

Mean grew tired—not surprising since Knavery had him pitching more innings this week than the entire Yankees pitching staff. He walked two to fill the bases. And when he hit Lynne and she didn't even cry, well, we knew he'd lost his stuff.

Knavery didn't really have a good backup pitcher. The score was 12–7. Our spirits were buoyed. Herm outdid himself with the rally caps: caps folded inside out, bills pointing skyward at forty-five-degree angles with a baseball cupped in each bill. "Superb job, Herm." Pity he had to bat.

Herm went to the plate wearing the catcher's shin guards. What the hell is *he* doing? We found out when he sort of . . . stepped *into* . . . the first pitch, which hit him on the shin guard, and the umpire let him go to first base, forcing in another run.

"What the hell is *that*?" Knavery shouted.

Jean "singled," if you will, driving the ball four feet in front of the plate, where nobody could get their hands on it.

It was 12–10 with Jean on first and Hermie on second. The fans were going wild, but there was one out and we had Anand and Monique coming to the plate, giving me a renewed sense of futility.

As Anand batted, so to speak, I talked with Monique. It wasn't exactly the kind of inspirational exhortation Knute Rockne used to give his players, but . . .

"You OK, Monique? Do you have to go to the bathroom or anything?"

"Mmm, no, not really," she replied, regarding this as a casual question.

"Well," I chuckled, "I noticed you downing that fifty-six-ounce Super Quencher, and naturally I thought, you know . . . I was just thinking that if you did actually . . . *have* to go, I would certainly understand. It would be all right . . . because, you know, *Emily* would be coming up to bat—and there wouldn't be all that *pressure* on you (not to mention your bladder) . . . worrying about making the Last Out Of The (whole goddamned) Season and everything."

"But, Mr. Geist, there's no bathroom here."

"I could have someone run you over to my house," I offered.

"That's pretty far."

(Exactly!)

"Not that far," I said.

We were both quiet for a while. Anand took strike two.

"You *know,* Mr. Geist," Monique said, "it's 12–

10, and we could still maybe *win* if I don't make the last out."

"No, no Monique, it's not that at all . . . I just. . . ."

"You know, Mr. Geist, I *really* have to go to the bathroom. Right now!" I squeezed her hand.

"Mom!" Willie screamed. He'd been monitoring the scene closely and instantly called for Monique's ride.

Anand struck out. Knavery's team cheered.

"Emily!" I shouted. "You're up."

Knavery checked his scorebook and charged onto the field. "Where's Monique! Monique is supposed to be up to bat."

I explained to Dick that Poor Little Monique has weak kidneys, "a kidney *problem,*" I called it. "I don't know if dialysis will be necessary," I told him, "Just removing the pressure may be enough. Remember Little Monique in your prayers, Dick."

"Bullshit!" Dick replied. And he held a team meeting on the mound. The meeting was meant to calm everybody down, but—face it—almost everything a coach says and does makes kids more nervous.

Emily scrunched down until her strike zone vanished completely and she drew a walk. She trotted slowly down to first base and then just took off wildly for second.

A team relaxes after a walk, and no one is paying much attention to what's going on. Mean Gene was strolling around the mound with his head down, wiping the sweat from his brow and kicking the pitching rubber. He looked up when his coaches began screaming! Six coaches can make a lot of noise. I didn't say a word. Frankly I couldn't quite comprehend what the hell was going on.

And Jean certainly had no idea. She was standing on second when she saw Emily coming, so she figured she'd better get the hell out of there. Hermie saw Jean coming to third and ran home. Mean Gene panicked and threw the ball to second base, where there was no one to catch it. Why would there be after a walk? At that moment it came clear to me how atomic bombs work. Emily had set off a chain reaction of monumental proportions—and with powerful destructive force.

I grabbed Anand, and squeezed him, watching as the ball went into center field, and Jean rounded third and headed for home plate. The center fielder threw the ball home, where—of course!—Jean was safe. Catchers can't be totally packed in safety gear and play baseball at the same time.

Emily darted to third, a runner possessed. The catcher fired the ball over the head of the third baseman into the service window of the Mr. Whippee truck.

Emily ran home through the darkness to score the winning run, and was mobbed at home plate in an eleven-player, one-coach, numerous-parent pileup.

Jean was so happy she kissed several of the boys on the mouth. Parents, some of them bombed on chardonnay, kissed me.

I saw Gerald Meeks, who'd quit on ethical grounds, jumping up and down. "I still can't figure out why that street light didn't come on," I said, hugging him.

He reached into his jacket pocket and gave me a quick glimpse of a pellet gun. "Knavery is a madman," he said. "He had to be stopped."

I kissed Gerald, on the lips, I think.

The Mr. Whippee man brought over the game ball. Jody ran up with Monique. I hugged Jody. I hugged Monique.

The team voted to give Monique the game ball.

THE WORLD SERIES
OF RIDGEWOOD

As champions of the West Side of town, we were honored (they said) to play the East Side champion in the Ridgewood World Series.

There was some bad blood between East and West. I've lived on both sides, been to the World Series with a team from each. The West Side has bigger houses; East-Siders think West-Siders are snobs. They love to just beat the hell out of the pampered West Side kids, and when they don't, they blame it on West-Siders having more money for better bats and gloves and batting instructors—or they might contend that West-Siders are typical Yuppie Type A's—young Ivan Boeskys and Michael Milkens—who insist their kids win at all costs or else.

On the other hand, when the West-Siders lose, they tend to blame it on the East-Siders' having nothing more important in their lives than how well their kids play baseball—people who insist that their kids win at all costs or else.

All of this is bullshit, of course.

Three days before the World Series, Emily called to say that she would not be able to make the World Series game because her entire family was leaving town on a trip.

Not Able To Make The World Series? Let me try to grasp that concept. Is that like: Not Able To Attend My Wedding? Not Able To Pick Up My Lottery Winnings?

I sat in stunned silence for the longest while. Emily thought we had been disconnected: "Mr. Geist?"

"May I. . . speak to your father?" I asked.

"Hello, Mr. Chang? Emily tells me you are going on a family trip and I appreciate the centrality of the family to your culture and everything, but we're talking here about missing the World Series. Do you know the centrality in our culture of the World Series! Couldn't the trip be postponed for a few days? I mean, a thousand pardons and everything but We'll Lose Without Emily. I mean, our two nations have always been friends, throughout the whole Mao thing. You're in America now and this is baseball, *the World Series!*"

"I am sorry, Mr. Geist. This has been arranged for some time. Our family is returning to Taipei."

"No problem," I said. "I'll drop her off there after the game."

We played an undefeated team from the East Side sponsored by Radon Busters. The backstop was bedecked with red, white and blue pennants. The Commissioner was there.

Everything was great, except: we had no pitcher. B.A. had pitched all six of his allotted innings against Knavery's team. Emily would have been our pitcher. Marcel pitched, admirably, and we held a 5–2 lead going into the bottom of the last inning, when he just couldn't pitch anymore and started walking everybody.

They tied the game up and had runners at second and third when I brought in Charlie to try his hand at pitching. He hadn't pitched since an early season fiasco. We decided to intentionally walk the next batter so we'd have a force out at every base, but during the intentional walk, Charlie threw a wild pitch, a run came in, and the East-Siders had beaten us 6–5.

The mother of one of the players on the opposing team is a friend of ours and practically every time I see her she reminds me that they beat us. Not unusual, except: the game was eight years ago. Last year, a team of mine won the Ridgewood World Series. I have been trying to befriend people on the opposing team so I can constantly remind them.

Some of my kids cried. I know we don't look terribly happy, posing with our runnerup trophies, because I still have the photograph.

Trophies are big business in America these days. Willie is older now and he has so many trophies he can't keep them in his room anymore. Most of them have been packed off to the basement. A friend of his had so many trophies that his shelf collapsed.

Foozle ordered the Little League World Series trophies. The winners' individual trophies were the same size and same color—no gold and silver differentiation—as the losers' trophies and both bear the same inscription: Ridgewood World Series Champions.

Maybe Barney did it on purpose so there'd be no hurt feelings—although ineptitude seems more likely. Maybe both teams are champions, as he would say in his saccharine way.

At any rate, the kids can display these trophies proudly in their rooms, and their friends can come over and look at them, and maybe one day Willie will show his trophy to his own children.

It will be up to each individual on that Curl Up 'N' Dye squad whether or not they confess the true outcome of the game. (Certainly they'll always remember it.)

They gave me one of the trophies, too. And I know what I'm saying.

Remember that draft pick you used to get a player with a swimming pool? Maybe he or she struck out in crucial situations to keep you out of first place and the playoffs. He or she may be the reason none of your players received trophies of any kind, and may be the reason so many parents in town think you stink as a coach and a human being. A losing record can lead to such things. Well, now is the time when that draft selection pays off.

The postseason party is at his or her house. At the party the coaches always give the kids a little something, and usually we get a little something from the kids, such as "I'm the Coach" T-shirts, which you can put out at the garage sale, but they won't sell. Believe me.

The only mementoes I've saved are a small plaque and a baseball that was signed by all the players on one of my teams. After our final game one year, my co-coach and I were presented with bottles of wine, which we opened in the parking lot of Van Dyke's ice cream parlor and consumed right then and there without benefit of cups. The Commissioner heard about it.

At the team party, I usually give to each team member a baseball or softball with some complimentary remark about the player written on it: "MVP"; "Home Run King"; "Best Batting Average"; "Fastest Runner"; "Team Sparkplug"—that type of thing.

With the worst of the players, like Anand and Monique, you really have to get creative: "Perhaps Most Improved"; "Usually on Time"—that sort of thing.

The pickup games we play at the postseason parties are almost always more fun than any of the games we play during the season, which tells you something. No pressure. No score-keeping. Play any position you want. Don't "work hard out there." Play.

ALL STARS

As coach of the West Side champion, I was again honored (they said), to be the coach of the West Side all-star traveling team.

Just when you think the season is finally over, your son or daughter brings home a note from the coach regarding tryouts for an all-star team, or congratulating you on your child's selection to the all-star team.

Of course, if you deny your child this opportunity, you will destroy his or her self-esteem. But you'll probably fall for it, too, hook, line and sinker. You're naturally proud of your child. You're flattered. You love saying at parties: "Well Timmy is on the traveling all-star team, and . . ." It's an offer you can't refuse.

No problem, just cancel your vacation. Do you think Mount Airy Lodge in the Poconos will give you back your five-hundred-dollar deposit? Suuurre they will!

There will be practices every day, and you will drive. Since this is an all-star team selected from far and wide, you will drive great distances.

There are stories in our town of mothers deliberately feeding their children right before swim team tryouts to give them cramps. They'd rather the kids *drowned* than make the swim team, which requires long-distance driving because of the scarcity of pool time.

We are members of the fifty-thousand-mile club. We get Christmas cards from the Garden State Parkway and New Jersey Turnpike Authority. My son can hook a quarter over the top of the car into the coin basket with agility and ease on the Garden State Parkway, because we've driven up and down those roads to basketball tournaments since the fourth grade.

There is a trend now to play all-star games all over the country. Third-grade soccer players go to Virginia, fifth-grade basketball players to Puerto Rico. "Where you going son?" you will ask. "Next door to Tommy's?" And he will reply: "Tierra del Fuego, Dad."

Three of my son's friends (one very good player, one of my son's caliber and one of a lesser caliber) played on an all-star baseball team last summer in France! Who the hell plays baseball in France?

To pay for these trips, the kids sell candy. To you. "Can I put you down for, say, *thirty* cases of peanut brittle, Dad?"

Whattya . . . takin' the Concorde?!

My son's AAU basketball team won about three games last year and he walks in the door and says they're the state champions and are going to the national finals in Memphis. When he was younger, we'd have done handsprings. Now we ask: how much is *this* going to cost?

But I have to admit, I've happened to mention in the course of conversations with friends and relatives and cashiers and the postman and toll collectors and anyone else who will listen: "Yeh, well, my son's in Memphis at the national AAU basketball finals and, um . . ."

We had been attending his basketball games for, oohhh, about seven or eight months one season (three seasons really: fall, winter, spring), and we found ourselves on the road in New Haven, Connecticut, *praying* they'd lose a game—if they won one more, they were going to Las Vegas. Nice place for kids. Plane tickets run about $800; hotels $150 a night, you know. High rollers. They lost by two points. A father on the other team said to me: "Kind of hard to say who really won that one, isn't it?"

You will find, as often as not, that the all-star coaches are Cro-Magnons who wanted to be Marines, but who couldn't pass the moral standards tests.

They will say things like: "The fun's over!" (or "*ovah,*" if they're in the New York metropolitan area, as we are).

They are here to win, to protect the good name of your town. They are tired of losing to those other towns, they may well mention that Road to Williamsport.

Your child will play in other towns in facilities that will amaze you.

There seems to be some inverse relationship between the wealth of a community and the quality of its baseball facility. The less well-to-do, blue-collar communities nearby have the finest sports facilities for kids; they may not have trash pickup, but could host the Olympic Games.

We arrive with our all-star team in a working-class town, looking for all the world like fatted calves going to slaughter. And what slaughter-houses! One town where we are regularly rendered has a baseball facility that is not only far more attractive than the town—but somewhat larger: four beautifully manicured baseball fields, with enormous light towers, stands for hundreds and thousands of fans, pro quality dugouts, snack bars serving not just Snickers bars but hamburgers, and nachos, for God's sake, restrooms, and public address systems.

The kids go bananas. The dugouts are so nice that I took Hermie along to see them, even though he was a long way from being an all-star.

The kids especially love hearing their names announced over the PA: "Rickeee Ziegel, Bill Walker . . ." Wow! Who cares if you lose! It's a pleasure.

Playing under the lights! On grass so green it looks painted.

Some towns even have the outfield fences with the advertisements painted on them—just like in minor league parks.

They all hold "fifty-fifty" games and these amazing raffles. You could *Win a Car* at the Little League game! These guys don't screw around!

The players on the other team look positively . . . salaried. And no problem with child labor laws, these kids look . . . old! They reek of aftershave. Their driver's licenses have been altered to say they're ten years old.

I live in a well-to-do suburb with painfully high property taxes yet most of our baseball fields are bumpy, some of them dangerously so. There are no bleachers at *any* of the fields. Want to watch our high school baseball team play? Sit on the ground. Most of our fields don't have dugouts. Maybe one out of ten has an outfield fence. No lights. No PA systems. No refreshments. At most fields there are actually not even benches for the *players* to sit on! What's the deal?

Frankly, as I look around at some of these facilities in other towns, I realize they'd never be able to build them in the center of our suburb. Because we use our baseball fields for soccer, lacrosse and other vaguely un-American activities. And we like our town to look manicured. Certainly that great outfield fence with the sponsors names on it would not be allowed. A little . . . *tacky,* don't you think? We want our upper-middle-class communities to look like an interior decorator did the outdoors. And as any kid knows: you can't really have any fun in a house where there's been an interior decorator.

You realize in these other towns that you are taking your all-star team into a gilded cage populated with hairy-legged, hairy-lipped monsters. And that's the girls' softball league. After one devastating loss to a pitcher who looked five years our kids' senior, I just went ahead and asked the pitcher when his birthday was. The kid did not say. His coach snapped "July 31," the cutoff date.

I usually find myself sitting next to some burly father of a kid on the opposing team. The father is encouraging his son: "What the hell you doin' up there, Bobby? Strike out again and don't bother comin' home!"

And guess what? Afraid of becoming homeless at age ten, Bobby does *not* strike out again. Great motivator. With the fear of God in him, Bobby hits a ball up into the light standards, a la *The Natural,* and the old man applauds. Not overly enthusiastically, mind you, this is what Bobby is *expected* to do.

I'm not overly enthusiastic in my praise either, not with the *power lifter* sitting next to me rooting for the other team. Question, sir: Do they actually *sell* anabolic steroids at the refreshment stand?

These are towns where you'd better drive an

American car to the game, thank you, and you'd better sing the national anthem like you mean it, buster!

I recall one August when Willie had been up at a camp all summer in New Hampshire, identifying trees and kayaking, and the *very next day* after he arrived home, he was given a football uniform and put into a scrimmage across from a tight end who was Growling! Really. It wasn't pretty.

It's a pretty heavy dose of reality.

Oh well, those Taiwanese will make short work of Bobby and his father.

But, don't you see, this is their chance. They turn around and look at you while they cheer. These Yuppies who look down on us; we'll kick their butts but good. The plumber can humble the CEO's son, send the investment banker home, to the nine-hundred-thousand-dollar home he bought with his last Christmas bonus, and make him dwell there in unhappiness because his son struck out. You can get to them that way.

Plumbers' revenge. Yes!

EPILOGUE

Here's what happens in the end: they stop. The kids just . . . stop playing baseball. Despite your dyspepsia, your yelling and screaming, they don't make the Yankees or the Cubs or the Dodgers at all! They stop, which is a good thing to keep in mind when you're out there on the Little League playing fields.

They can't hit the curve ball, or the coach at the next level is a dork, or they're second string, or they suddenly—"Hey!"—realize: "I don't even like this game anymore!" or they like soccer or lacrosse or hanging out at the mall with their friends better. This generally pisses off the old man at least a little bit. "Throwin' in the towel, eh kid?"

Willie is sixteen now and he has stopped. He wasn't quite the hitter he thought he should be and didn't like the game enough to work at it. He was one of the very best baseball players of his age in town, and last year for the first time since he was eight years old he didn't play organized baseball. He decided to keep playing in basketball leagues until July. Gene, the best pitcher in town, did the same thing. Mark, perhaps the best all-around baseball player in town, joined the tennis team. They just stop.

In the end, Willie has turned out to be the high school athlete I was not, and I guess that's part of what I was after. Send him back to clear up that unfinished business for me. He received a varsity basketball letter as a sophomore. He is a captain of the football team. I never made the teams.

One night a couple of years ago, when he was fourteen, there was a big teen-age beer party next door. Willie and one of his friends were out in our driveway around 11 P.M. shooting baskets and keeping an eye on the revelers when Big Dave Reynolds, two years his senior, the hero of one of Willie's undefeated baseball teams crashed through the bushes, completely inebriated, and began loudly reminiscing about those golden days on that indomitable—almost Taiwanese-like!—team.

I saw a photograph in the newspaper last year of another boy from town who was never quite as good as Willie and who was playing on some Team U.S.A. or other in Europe. I guess I still believe that if I'd insisted Willie live at the batting cage, insisted that he be a pitcher even though he didn't want to be, that he'd be an awfully good baseball player right now, maybe even good enough to . . . well, never mind. Let it go.

He has baseball in proper perspective. He and the other kids always did; for the adults, particularly the fathers, it has taken longer.

My daughter still plays softball. I still coach. My son didn't make it to the Yankees, so I guess she probably won't either. I can calm down a bit.

I think I'm finally starting to get it now, starting to understand. So, it really *is* just a game, huh? And if it's not being played for fun, why play at all? To learn values? That's asking a lot of a game. Play for fun and they'll learn the values, I think. Come to think of it, that *is* a value.

After all the years of organized and highly disorganized baseball, I'll take the disorganized, thanks, without benefit of adult supervision. Give me a good pickup game on a Sunday afternoon with kids of all ages. We've had a couple in recent years, but for the most part when the organized leagues are finished with the diamonds, the grass grows on the basepaths in short order.

Or a game with my wife and two kids in the backyard can be good. Since the teams are rather small, we sometimes allow our two cats to play in the field. They like to chase the ball. If either cat pounces on the ball before the runner reaches first base, the runner is out.

Sometimes Willie and I go over to a local diamond and I hit him towering fly balls, which he catches—in dramatic fashion—against the outfield fence, sometimes leaping to rob me of a home run. (Sometimes they go over the fence and he has to do battle with a pit bull's cousin to retrieve them.) He's probably still pretending that he's Winfield or some updated version of Winfield on a highlight reel; I'm pretending to be Stan Musial or Jose Canseco.

And we still play catch in the yard, my son and

I. But it's more pleasant now. No more expectations, no judgments, no instruction, no disapproval, no hard feelings.

Just a game of catch. He is careful not to throw the ball too hard.